ART SPARKS

IDEAS. METHODS. PROCESS.

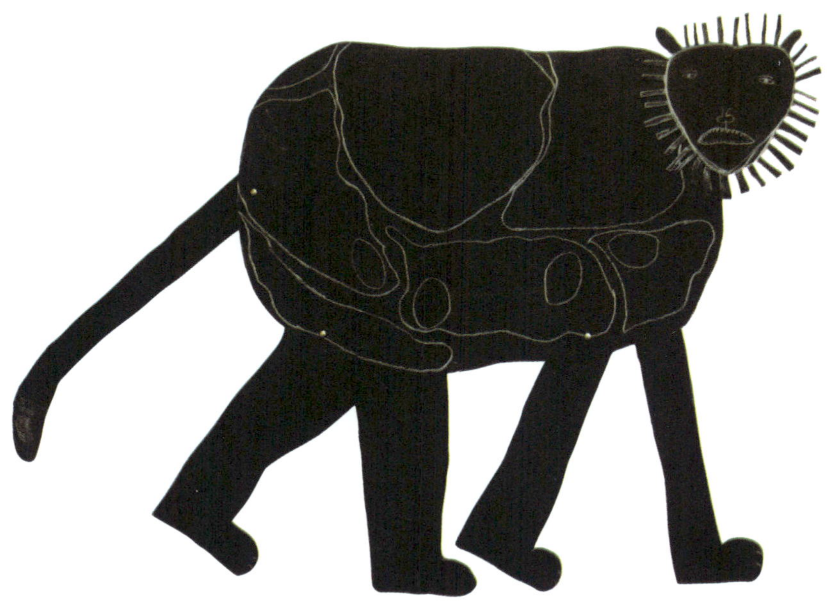

Nisha Nair

CONTENTS

INTRODUCTION

For those of us in the field of art education, the motivations for what we do stem from an unwavering belief in the value of art and its impact on children's learning. Art is essential to the growth and development of all children. Research indicates that sustained art-making contributes to the development of valuable thinking skills and attitudes such as the ability to pose questions, test ideas, apply judgment, take creative risks, solve artistic problems, think flexibly and divergently, and deal with uncertainty. Art also fosters the development of creativity, a critically important skill for success in the 21st century. Furthermore, art offers a space within which children can explore new ideas, advance their thinking, and apply the insights gained towards their own art-making.

In spite of its many contributions, art is often considered secondary within the school curriculum. If not completely excluded, it's treated as an extra perk for those with talent as opposed to a necessity for all, a term reserved for subjects such as math, science, and language. Or it's seen as an opportunity to temporarily relieve stress from the rigorous curriculum. While a few schools offer art as a core subject, important by itself, and made available to all children, many schools defend the presence of art in the school-day curriculum by pointing to the support it can lend to those subjects deemed more important. Art in these instances merely serves to illustrate content in other subject areas. Such secondary purposes assigned to art often justify its omission when other subjects require more attention, which in turn ensures its marginalisation.

On the other hand, many attempts have been made to advocate for the inclusion of art within schools across India. Discussions regarding the value of art in education, by those who support it, emphasise how art enables children to express feelings and emotions freely, enhances children's senses and develops aesthetic appreciation, builds their understanding of cultural heritage and diversity, makes them good, creative citizens, and helps them acquire an understanding of formal art techniques such as the principles and elements of design (NCERT, 2010). Discussions also emphasise the need for a flexible curriculum that leverages the value of integrating the arts, and other such "co-curricular" subjects, with the regular curriculum (Draft National Education Policy 2019—mhrd.gov.in/sites/upload_files/mhrd/files/nep/English1.pdf). Despite this, recommendations to make art a compulsory subject in every school up to the 10th standard have not been fully realised (NCERT, 2010; 2005).

The problem perhaps has to do with how we talk about art in education. Current perceptions of art in India are often shaped by a range of beliefs: an artist is someone who is naturally skilled and possesses inborn talent in drawing and/or painting; not everyone possesses talent in art; teaching art is about teaching technical skill; a creative person is someone who draws well; art cannot be taught and teaching art stifles creativity; art-making is solely about feelings and emotions, not analysing, reasoning, evaluating. It is important to recognise that these beliefs are based on narrow conceptions of art, and can be problematic. Oftentimes, it is these beliefs that continue to marginalise the presence of art within the school curriculum.

Given that art can play a powerful role in enriching children's learning, changing problematic perceptions of art, and validating its role in education, seems imperative. This also means that we rethink the ways we speak about art, and focus on how it enriches a child's thinking skills and attitudes, creating an impact that extends well beyond the art classroom.

This is what this book aims to do.

The Context

This book presents the work conducted with a group of 6th standard students (11 years of age) at a low-cost aided private school situated in a rural village in the Kolar District of Karnataka. The school serves children many of whom are first-generation school-goers. It has a committed management, principal and team of teachers, as well as cooperative parents eager to see their children receive a well-rounded education. While the principal and teachers have to cope with a heavy State-prescribed syllabus, and limited time to cover it, there is growing recognition amongst them that student learning should include more than just rote memorisation for the purpose of test-taking. Some of the strategies that the teachers utilise to help promote student understanding include enacting topics, using pictures to encourage discussions, and using modelling to demonstrate new concepts. In an effort to address classroom challenges, the teachers and the principal are eager to engage with new ideas and strategies through professional development opportunities: strategies that can help raise the motivations and outcomes of their students. It is in this context that they welcomed the art interventions which form the subject of this book.

The Children

32 children, comprising both girls and boys, participated in the 12-session programme intent on engaging them in enriching arts-based learning through the media of drawing and puppet-making. The children were no strangers to art. However, their experiences making art were limited to the occasional drawing (reproducing existing illustrations from books) and craft activity (creating Rangoli-like surface decorations with seeds, for example). This was going to be their first experience working on a multi-step art project, culminating in the creation of shadow puppets.

Preliminary observations of the children revealed that they were used to a culture of seeking teacher approval and making things look 'correct.' The intensity of these behaviours varied amongst children, but in general they were visible amongst the majority. The children were also English language learners. While all of them were proficient in Kannada, their English language abilities varied. Some children had a higher level of English comprehension. Others were challenged due to limited vocabulary knowledge and comprehension, which in turn impacted their confidence to use the language. The challenge was to engage with these realities and see if children's participation in an arts-based programme would help change behaviours, boost confidence, foster independent thinking, as well as impact their ability to respond to their artworks and speak about them effectively.

The Art Experience

The planned art experience carried out over 12 sessions comprised a series of lessons, in the course of which children created their own imaginary hybrid animal puppets. The lessons were devised keeping in mind the learning proclivities and needs of 11-year olds. Children in this age group are more sensitive to the opinions of others and self-conscious about their artistic abilities. They are interested in learning how to depict things as they know them to be in the world around them. So, for example, when tasked with drawing a horse, they want their drawings to look like a real horse, and are often dissatisfied if they don't. But children in this age group are also capable of making conceptual leaps, and when given the opportunity, can explore the fantastical as much as they can explore things rooted in the real world.

Given these two seemingly contrary ways in which children respond and understand the world, the 12-session programme worked at two levels. The first level comprised observational drawing components and strategies that broke down complex animal forms into simple shapes. The intention was to help develop children's capacity to look closely, trust their eyes, and more confidently capture what they see before them. The second level comprised an imaginative component—the creation of imaginary hybrid animals.

The connection to animals in general, a subject that all children are familiar with, helped ensure that the unit was relevant and applicable to children from diverse settings.

A primary goal of each lesson was to go beyond a singular focus on skill development in art—to include the development of valuable thinking skills and attitudes in the children that participated.

Furthermore, this sequence of lessons also encouraged the development of communication skills in the children, helping foster personal self-expression. For language learners, English language learners in this instance, the lessons provided several opportunities to acquire new vocabulary, participate in group dialogues and reflections, as well as engage in writing. The imaginary hybrid animal puppets lent themselves to the development of simple written character sketches. The puppets also lent themselves to the creation of simple stories. Engaging with language in a fun and interactive manner enables children to shed inhibitions, normally associated with acquiring a new language, which in turn serves as a first step towards building confidence and competence in that language.

The Book

This book deconstructs the in-class sessions and presents key ideas explored in the process of the children's art-making. It uses concrete examples to reveal how impactful learning can be promoted in the art classroom, and the significance of this learning on children's overall growth and development. In doing so, it challenges some of the popular conceptions held regarding art and the teaching of art. By the same token, it offers the reader an alternative perspective that speaks to the central role that art can and should play in children's education.

In the quest to create enriching learning opportunities that expand children's thinking, developing them into curious, reflective, engaged learners, this book offers tools that can be used to create learning interventions, rooted in art that engages, enables, and inspires.

This book is intended for all those who are concerned with children's education - parents, teachers of all subjects (including art), artists, school administrators, policy makers - and those curious about the role of art in education.

Keeping in mind the artistic development of children, the learning experiences featured in this book are best suited for children from 5th to 7th standard.

They have been arranged in a sequence of 4 sections, with each section devoted to a particular aspect of art learning. Within a section there are chapters that have to do with specific art lessons. Built into the chapters are useful pedagogic asides to the teacher, placed at the end of a page and appropriately framed by a horizontal orange bar. Two summaries end each chapter, the one consolidating all that has been learned about art, and the other, important details to do with the learning process.

It should be noted here that the term "art" used throughout this book refers to the visual arts, which in its broadest sense includes drawing, painting, collage, sculpture, puppet-making, printmaking, design, as well as the media arts such as photography and animation. While other forms of art (e.g. performing arts) undoubtedly have their own value, the focus of this book is on the visual arts.

The Author

I've spent 15 years working in the field of art education. 15 years of engaging artists, community members; teachers, education administrators, and most importantly, children. Of all these experiences, walking into a school and engaging children continues to be the most exhilarating. The enthusiasm of the children I encounter is infectious. And the thought of engaging young minds, helping unlock their capacities to imagine possibilities through art is immensely gratifying. Through the pages of this book, I invite you to step into an art classroom within a school in rural and Southern India, and experience what I experienced, observe what I observed as students engaged in the process of art-making.

LEARNING IN AND THROUGH ART

LEARNING IN AND THROUGH ART

Stretch, Explore, Discover

What do children learn through art, and what is the value of what they're learning?

In order for us to grow, we need repeated opportunities to reach beyond our normal capabilities and comfort levels. Reaching beyond, or the act of "stretching", requires us to be open, curious and ready to discover new possibilities.

Artists are known to thus go beyond what they know. Looking to enrich their practice, they pursue new directions and continuously explore materials and ideas. This process of stretching and exploring is enabling.

Along the way, artists learn that mistakes or accidents which happen when they venture into unfamiliar terrain are really valuable opportunities to grow and learn.

Children too need similar opportunities to grow. But our education system, with its excessive focus on covering large amounts of curriculum in a short period of time, makes it hard for children to explore and discover. The art classroom can help balance their learning process, by offering children the chance and openings to go beyond what they know, think and do.

What is Art?

My group of 11-year olds were no strangers to art. But their experiences in making art were limited. They could draw, but often copied existing illustrations from books. They did some craft activity—such as creating Rangoli-like surface decorations with seeds. This was going to be their first experience with a set of interconnected art lessons.

I decided to start with an activity that would help children use their observation skills. I had brought to class a selection of images, of varied art works. I asked the children look at them carefully and then posed my first question.

What is art?

I pointed to an image and wondered aloud:

Is this art?

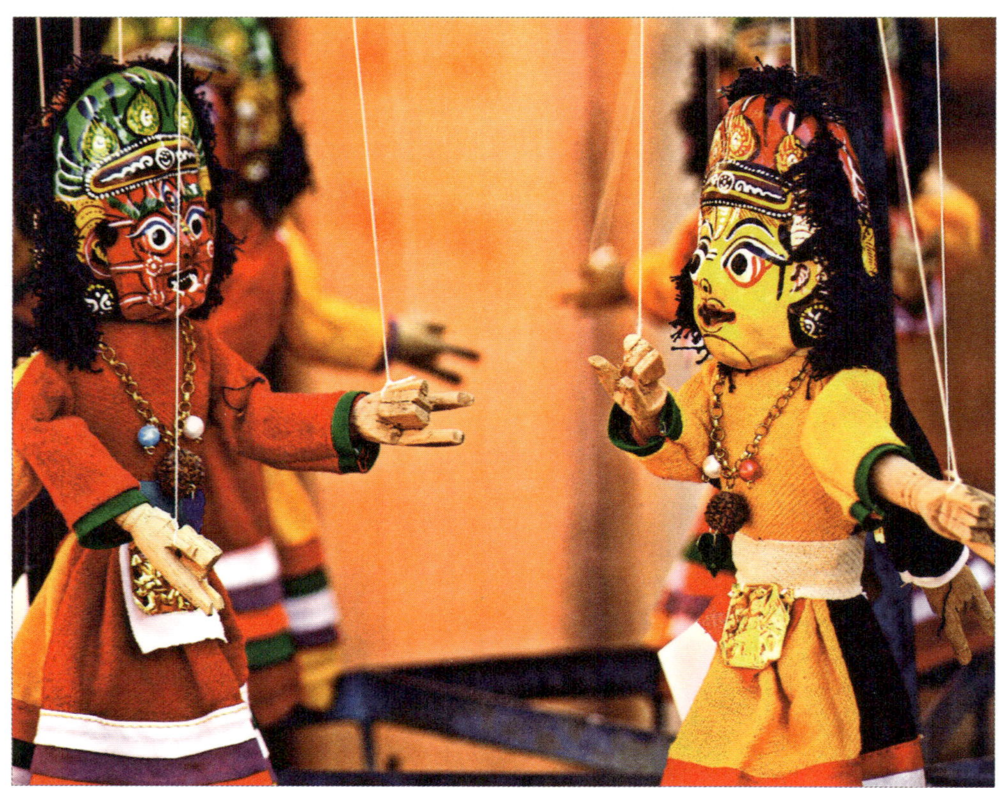

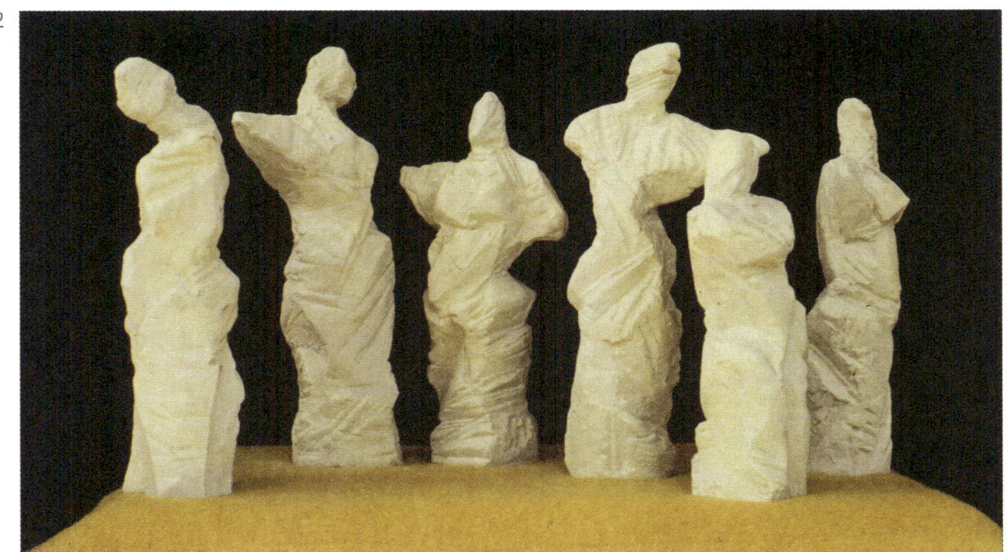

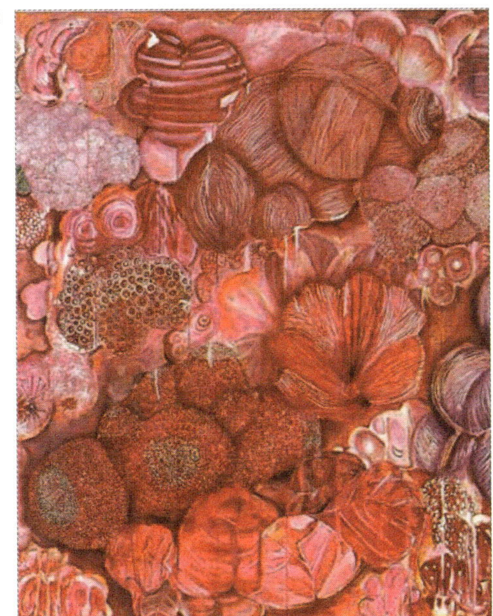

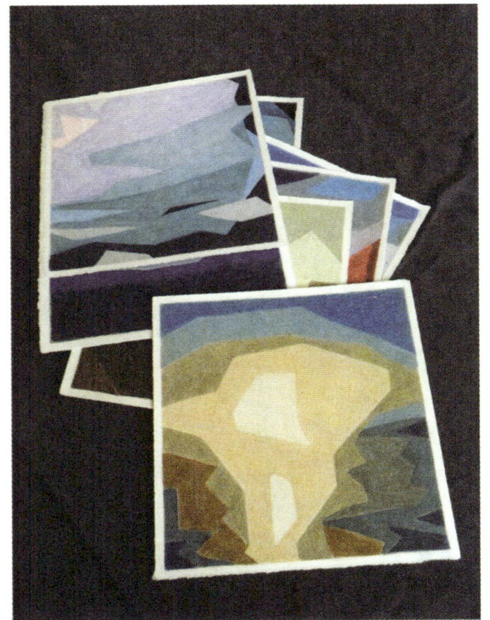

When selecting art reproductions to share with children, as an introduction to art, carefully pick a variety: realistic, abstract, traditional, non-traditional, two-dimensional, three-dimensional. This exposure to a range of artworks can help push the boundaries of children's thinking, and expand their ideas about art.

And added:

Why do you think this is art?

I wanted the children to loosen up, voice their opinions freely, consider different perspectives, and expand their understanding of art, and also what art could be.

The children offered a range of responses. Observing the vivid colours in some of the images shared, one child pointed out,
"Art has lot of colours."

Another pointed at a photograph that featured white sculptures and voiced her opinion:
"But art is also black and white."

I then asked:

Is art only about colour?

To which the children unanimously responded,
"Art has designs."

I encouraged the children to tell me why they thought so. I requested that I wanted more children in the class to respond—not just the same few who were always eager to share. Some pointed to the Kolam patterns, while tracing the curves of the patterns with their fingers. Others gestured at the decorative details in the picture of the string puppet that I had shared.

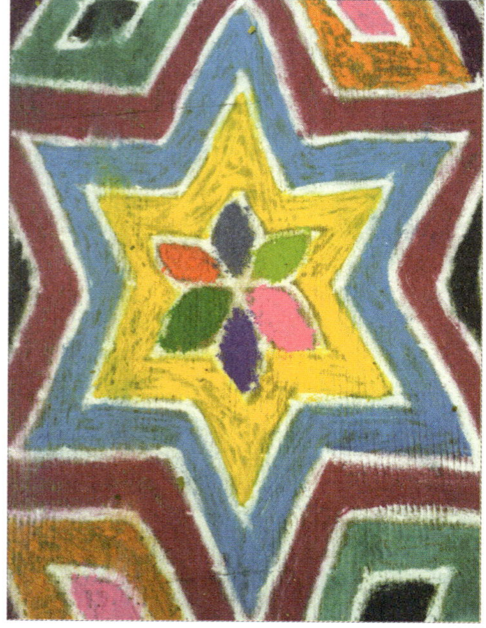

5

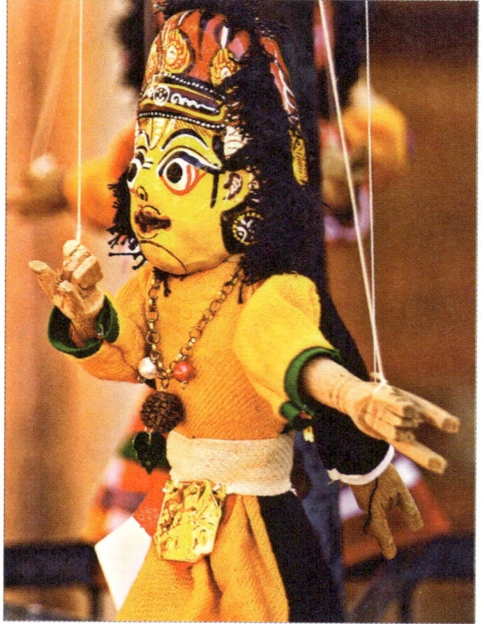

6

I then pointed to two other images on display, one of a contemporary painting on canvas and the other a painting on a wall.

Can you tell me what you see here?

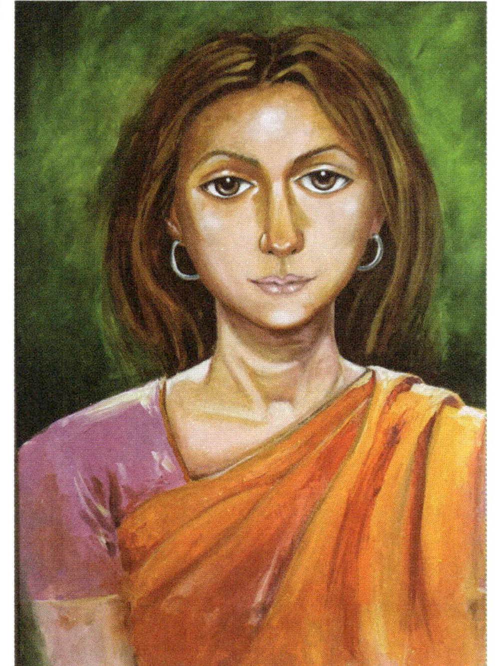

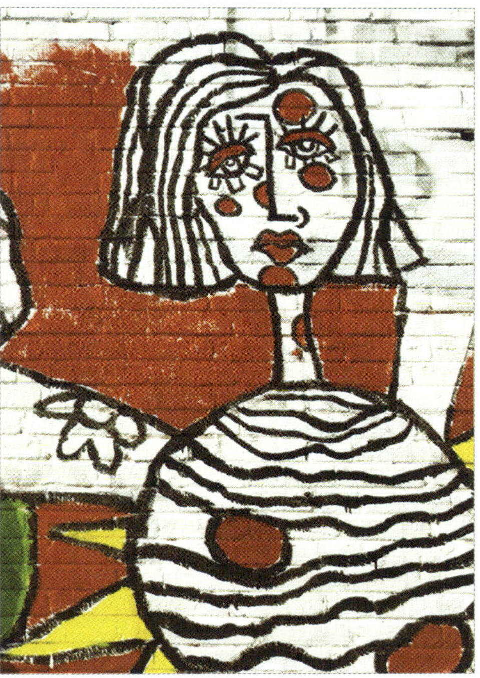

"Both are paintings."

Do you see any similarities between the two?

"They are using colours!"

"They are using green."

"[The] two paintings are showing people."

Look closer: are there any differences between the two paintings?

"One painting is [on] paper. Other painting is painting on a wall."

A child pointed to the painting on canvas and noted thoughtfully, "The woman in [this] painting looks real."

She then added:
"The woman in [the wall] painting is not real. [Her] face [does] not look real. It has many designs."

Why do you think this woman looks real?

I said, gesturing towards the painting on canvas.

A child called attention to the different skin tones and said,
"[Her] skin is like all people. Here it is light. Here all it is dark."

Do you see any other differences between the two paintings?

A child pointed to the wall painting and said,
"This one has lines, while that one has full colour."

The child had actually distinguished a 'line drawing' from
a more 'realistic' one, created by using colours.

Before we ended this part of our discussion on art, I made it
clear to the children that all their responses were valid, and that
there was no single right answer. However, I pointed out, every
response had to be based on what a child had noticed and
observed, in short, on evidence.

I then went back to a question I had posed earlier,
but with reference to the wall painting.

Why do you think the painting on the wall is art?

The children responded quickly:
"It is a beautiful picture!"

"It has many designs."

"It has beautiful colour!"

The children's responses made it clear to me that, like many others,
they considered colour, design and details as important features of
a work of art.

As long as most of these criteria were met, it did not seem to matter
if the painting was on a canvas or on a wall; whether it was realistic,
or more abstract.

We then looked at the remaining images.
I pointed to the photo of the sculpture and asked:

Is art just drawing and painting? Can it be a sculpture?
Looking at this image, what do you think a sculpture is?
How is a sculpture different from a painting?

The children came up with a range of responses. This indicated their growing capacity to look for clues in the artworks, which could provide them with more information.

"The sculpture is taller than [the] building."

"You [can] see it from [the] front and back.
 [But] a painting [you] can only see from [the] front."

"People can walk inside [the] sculpture."

What material has been used to create this sculpture?

"This is made of steel because [it] is outside.
 So even if it rains, it is not spoiled."

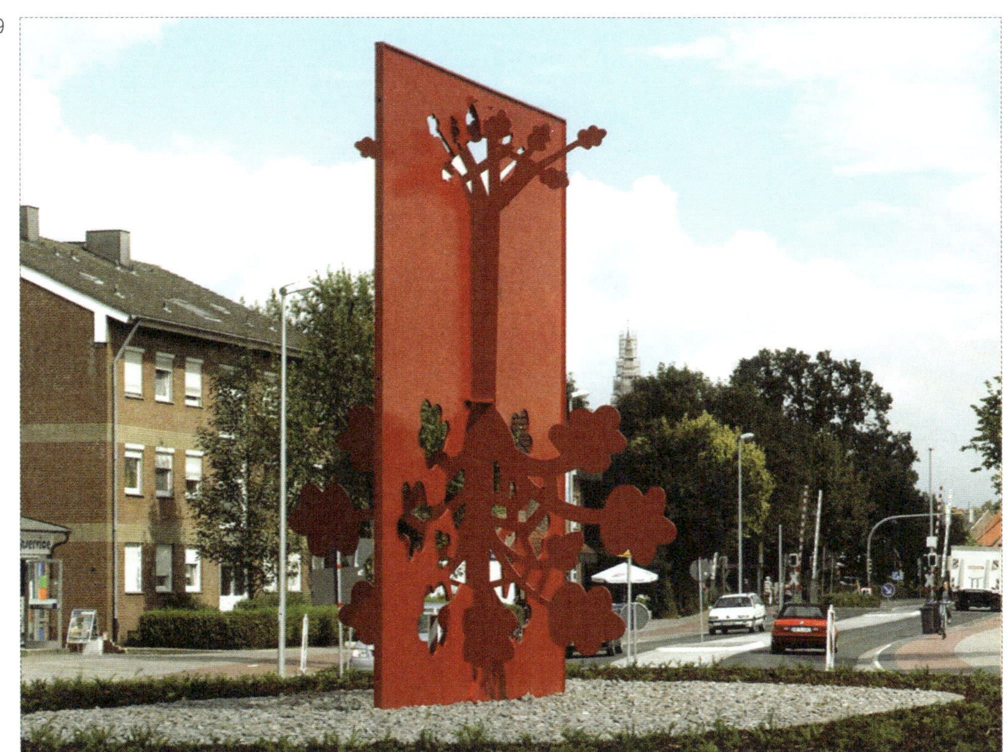

I pointed out:

So now we know that art can be made from all kinds of materials. Sometimes, these are common art materials such as paint. Sometimes these are materials found in nature. And, at other times, you can create art from everyday materials that you find around you.

I then pointed to the work of an artist - Hadieh Shafie - who uses quilling techniques (rolling strips of coloured paper) to create abstract, circular surface patterns.

What do you think this artwork is made of?

Pointing to the circular patterns in the artwork, a child said:
"Coloured carroms."

Her response indicated her openness to the fact that art can indeed be made of found and everyday objects. And, it also reflected her ability to connect what she was seeing with an object that she was very familiar with—in this case, a carrom. In the process, she had understood the artwork better.

10

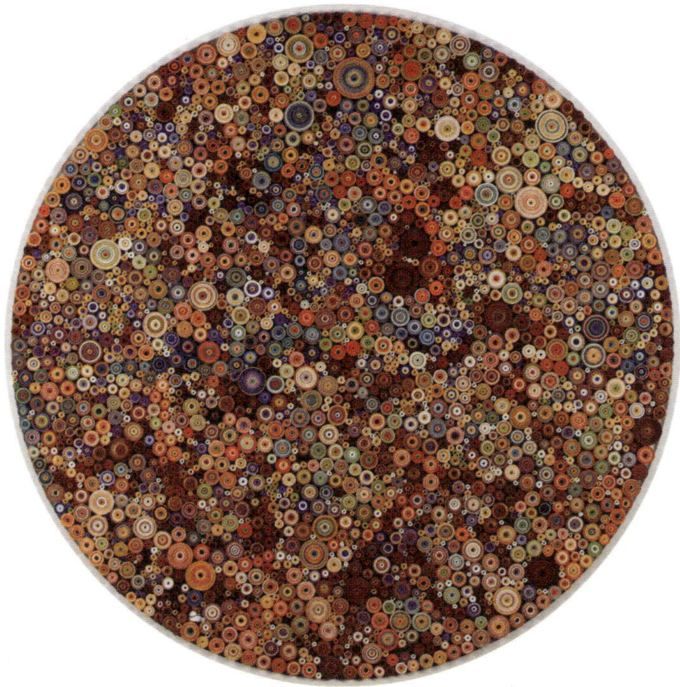

When introducing art vocabulary (e.g. observation, sculpture, materials, etc.) introduce no more than 4 new words in a given session. This gives children ample opportunities to grasp the new words introduced and use them in context without being overwhelmed.

These discussions made it apparent that the children were expanding on their notions of art. Since I had made it clear there were multiple ways of interpreting and responding to art, they had gained confidence in stating their opinions.

Most importantly, they were beginning to construct their own ideas about art, using evidence to support what they were saying. This was distinctly different from their usual tendency to rely on the teachers' answers.

I decided therefore that, going forward, I would allocate at least 10 minutes at the start of each lesson, for arts-based discussions. It seemed to me that such discussions would foster the development of skills and attitudes based on observation, reasoning and self-expression. And if children had sufficient experiences of this kind, they would be able to apply the same thinking processes to other situations, especially when they had to make sense of new information and experiences. In turn, this would go a long way in developing children into thoughtful, independent thinkers.

To support children that are English language learners, and facilitate their learning, the teacher can help translate classroom discussions from English to the students' native language, and vice versa. This allows students to move fluidly between two languages, gradually acquiring the new language, without compromising on their understanding. This strategy helps create an inclusive classroom environment, one in which all children have the opportunity to participate in discussions.

About Art

Popular views held about art and what it entails are often limiting. An inordinate emphasis on realistically rendered drawings and paintings, for example, often diminishes the richness and varied dimensions of artistic practice. In truth, artistic practice stretches across materials, forms, genres, whether realistic or abstract, literal or conceptual. Exposing children to the breadth of artistic practice ensures that they remain open and accepting of all the possibilities that art has to offer. It also emboldens them in their own art-making as they recognise that skillful rendering is not the only pre-requisite to being an artist. Allowing children to formulate their own interpretations of what they're seeing as they engage with art also helps remove the veneer of inaccessibility that often shrouds the viewing of art.

About the Learning Process

Traditional views of the teacher as the repository of all knowledge, imparting information to students who passively receive it, has been rightfully challenged. Yet, this is a view that's still prevalent in many circles. And, even in instances where more active modes of instruction are being championed, adopting close-ended questioning techniques does little to advance children's learning and understanding. They serve merely to obtain the correct answer and evaluate children's capacity to recall specific information learned.

In classroom environments where learning is seen as a dynamic and interactive process, questioning techniques, used appropriately, encourage children to think as they formulate their own responses, ask questions of their own, recognise and embrace diverse points of view, and develop deep understanding. The art classroom provides a wonderful space within which such valuable learning can be promoted.

A classroom that promotes inquiry is one where:

- Open-ended questions that allow for multiple answers are routinely posed to help stimulate children's thinking and elicit diverse responses. Inviting more than one response builds in children an awareness that questions often do not have just one right answer.

- Open-ended questions are planned by the teacher ahead of time, and align with the learning goals of the lesson.

- Children are given the time to formulate their answers and ask additional follow-up questions.

- Children are given the opportunity to back up their answers with evidence, learning to justify their thinking.

- Listening is encouraged.

- All children are engaged, not just the few that are always ready to answer.

- Teacher gently guides children who do not respond with the help of clues and prompts. The teacher also redirects children if needed to help stay on topic.

- Children's questions are often answered with another question to encourage children to think for themselves.

Mapping Ideas

Most people, when they begin on a drawing, try to make it look 'perfect' from the start. This notion of perfection often gets in the way of their ability to develop ideas freely. It's the same for children. Scared of making a mistake, children often use their erasers a lot. So much so, that some of them don't get to start on their drawing. Their anxiety at something not turning out 'perfect' ends up interfering with their ability to test out ideas.

Keeping these challenges in mind, I introduced the idea of mapping in the first session. I began by showing the class an example of a preliminary sketch and a finished painting.

Look closely at these two images. What's the difference between them?

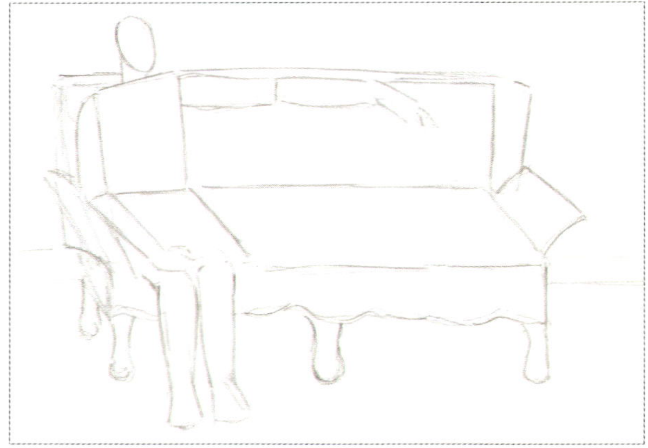

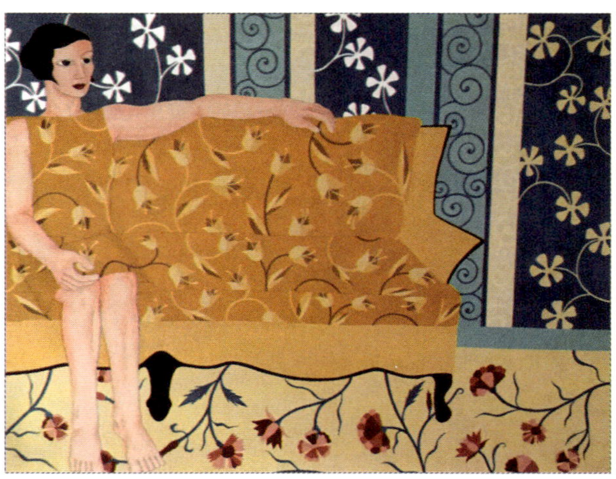

"This is black and white. It is drawn in pencil".

"This other painting is fully in colour."

**The black and white picture is called a sketch.
How else is it different from the painting?**

"It doesn't show all the parts!"

"There's a person sitting. But it doesn't show if it's a man or a woman."

They were referring to the fact that in the sketch, many of the identifiable details were missing. To prompt them further, I brought out a finished drawing in addition to the sketch.

What do you see in this drawing? Are the lines different from the sketch?

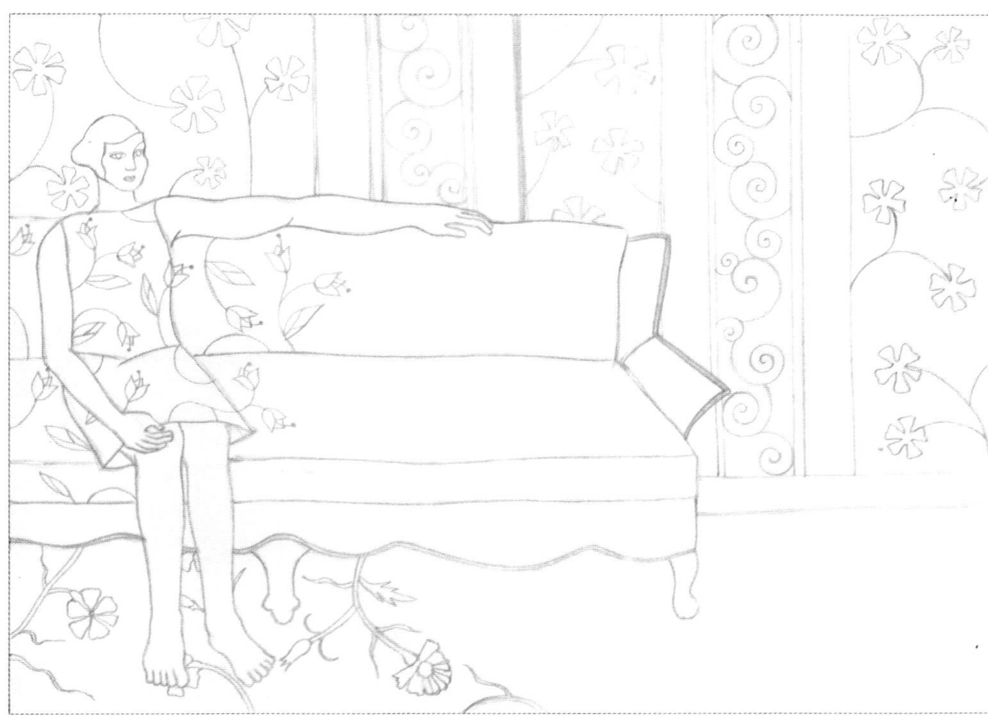

"The sketch has broken lines. The lines in the drawing are nice!"
Said an observant child, alluding to the fluid, continuous lines in the finished drawing.

**Do you think the artist started with the sketch?
Or did she start with the drawing?**

"Sketch!"
They said unanimously.

Why do you think the artist started with a sketch?

I asked this question to encourage the children to use their reasoning skills.

One child responded:
"[To] help to show the size of [a] person."

I was impressed with the child's response, she had grasped at something important, that artists often use sketches to plan size relationships.

Another responded:
"So she will not take time to finish [her] drawing and not like it."

This child had understood a valuable art practice: the quick study, which is something that artists do, before they decide which course to pursue to complete their artwork.

I compared the sketch to the drawing once more:

Are the lines in the sketch dark or light?

"Light."

Why do you think the lines in the sketch are light?
Why not start with dark lines?

"Light lines means [it's] easy to change."

Our discussions had helped the children understand that a sketch was a quick way of mapping out ideas—to do with size, shape and various other elements. They had learned that sketching was a great way to get started and test out ideas, without spending too much time on the details. They had also understood the difference between a sketch and a drawing: that a sketch was a framework on which a drawing could be developed, while a drawing was likely to be more refined and detailed. I re-introduced these ideas again later, across key sessions that involved sketching and drawing.

About Art

Drawing can be overwhelming for many people. Children, especially preteens and teenagers, tend to think that their drawings need to look a certain way. When they're uncertain about where and how to begin, they either limit themselves to the one or two things they know how to render, or end up creating simplified representations of what they're attempting to draw—using a stick figure to show the human body, for example. And as frustrations mount, due to their inability to draw things as they want them to be, many children give up. As a precursor to drawing, it is good therefore to introduce the concept of rough, exploratory sketching. This is a tool artists use to experiment and create quick studies. Crucially, this helps free children's hands and minds, and jumpstart creation.

About the Learning Process

The importance of freeing students from inhibitions - that restrict learning - can't be emphasised enough. You can use a variety of classroom practices to embolden them. One would be to guide them to work in manageable stages—where they can go from the simple and rough to more complex and refined. This helps to alleviate anxiety and encourages them to feel capable, as was the case with my 6th standard students. Working in stages gave them the confidence to start with quick sketches, and build on them to create detailed drawings. Encourage children to embrace imperfections: it's a necessary part of the learning process, which helps them to rethink and revise initial plans. This also helps them stay open to various possibilities and to test them out.

Lines and Shapes are Everywhere!

Following our discussions on how to map out ideas, I invited the children to look around the room to notice something else:

What types of lines do you see around you?

There was a prolonged pause, so I came up with an example of my own. I pointed to the window:

I see a straight, vertical line in the window grill!
What other kinds of lines do you see in this room?

This gave the children the little push they needed to start identifying lines themselves.

Some of their responses were obvious:
"I see straight lines in [the] blackboard."

Other observations were more unusual.
Indicating the folds on her classmate's dress, a child said:
"Wavy line in [her] uniform."

Another pointed to the backrest of a chair,
"I can see zigzag lines!"

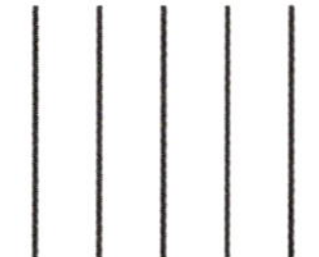 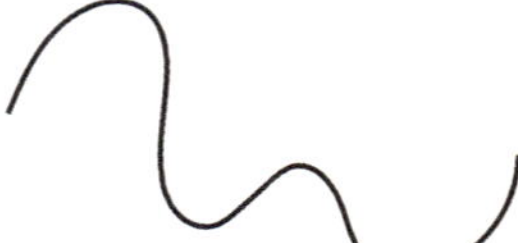 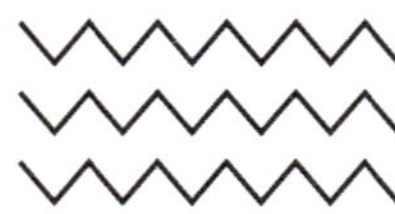

We moved on to shapes.

Look around the room! What shapes do you see?
How many types do you know? What shape is the clock?

"[The] clock is a circle."

"[The] table leg is [a] rectangle."

"[The] blackboard is a big rectangle!"

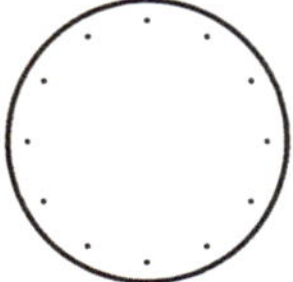 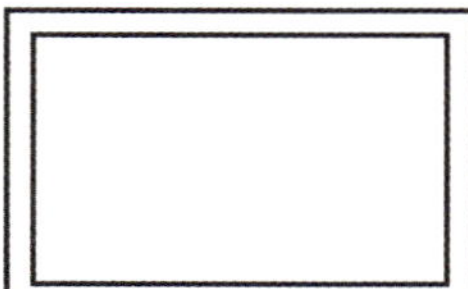

By asking them to look around and observe in this pointed way,
I wanted the children to recognise that lines and shapes are everywhere,
and that they are the basis of all form. With the help of a few prompts
the children began to realise that they themselves were made up of
a series of lines and shapes.

"My head is oval,"
    One of them said.

"Neck is a rectangle..."

"Ears are half-circles."

"Eyebrows have many thin lines."

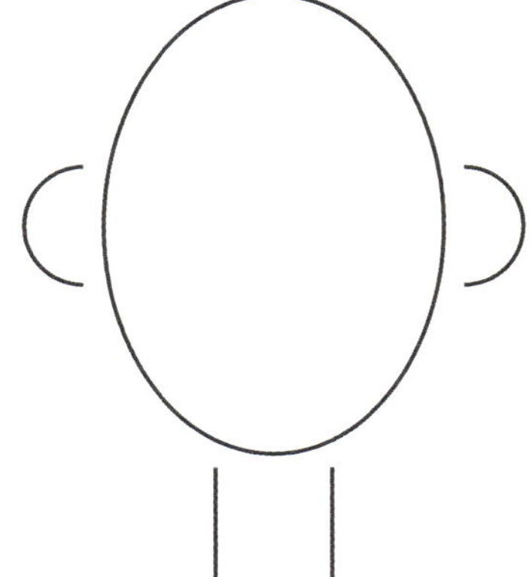

To reinforce what they had discovered through observation,
I began the demonstration part of the lesson by first introducing
the goals of the lesson:

Today we will create sketches of animals.
But first I want you to look carefully at some photos of animals.

Here's a picture of a buffalo. What lines and shapes do you see
in this photo? For example, what's the shape of the buffalo's head?

"[The] buffalo's face is a triangle."

11 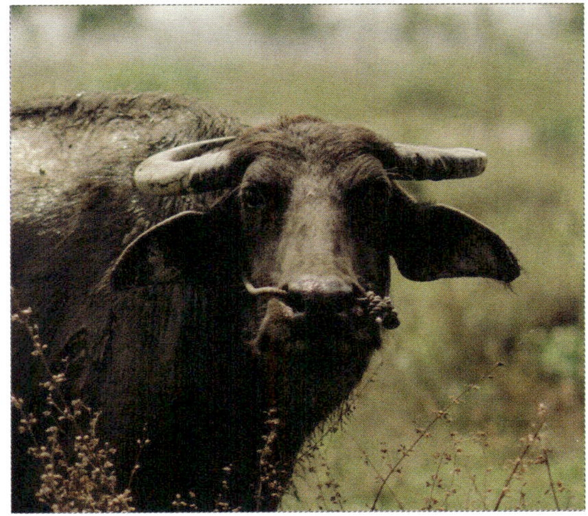

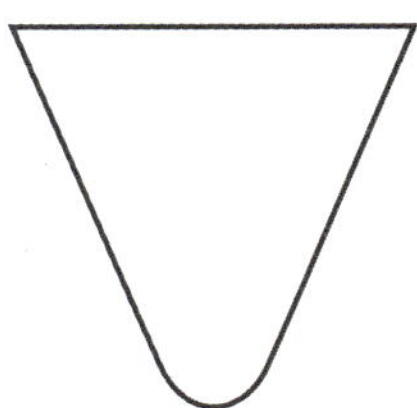

Preparing to sketch the buffalo, I asked:
What shape should I use for its body?

A child responded:

I pressed further:
How about its legs?
What shapes can I use to sketch the legs?

I used the children's suggestions to start sketching.
As I sketched, the children continued to point out details
about the buffalo. They drew on what they already knew
about lines and shapes, as they 'helped' me out.

I worked lightly with a pencil. From time to time, I looked closely at
the image of the buffalo, to double check the lines and shapes I was
sketching. I was "modelling" both the sketching process and the use
of close observation and wanted them to notice how I mapped
out the animal's form.

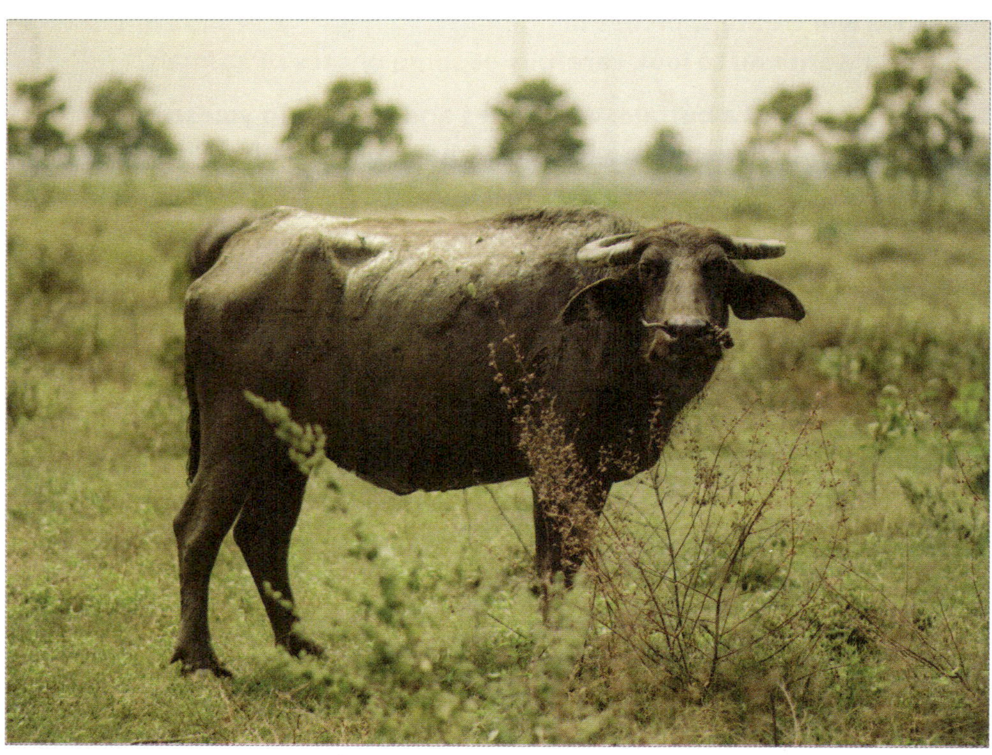

12

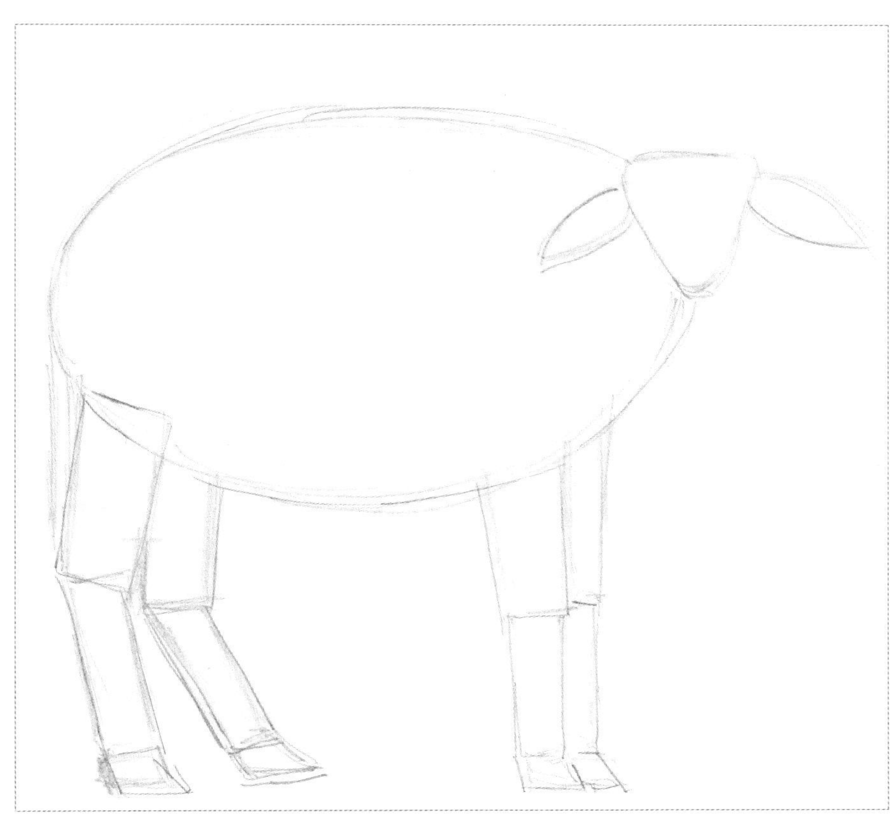

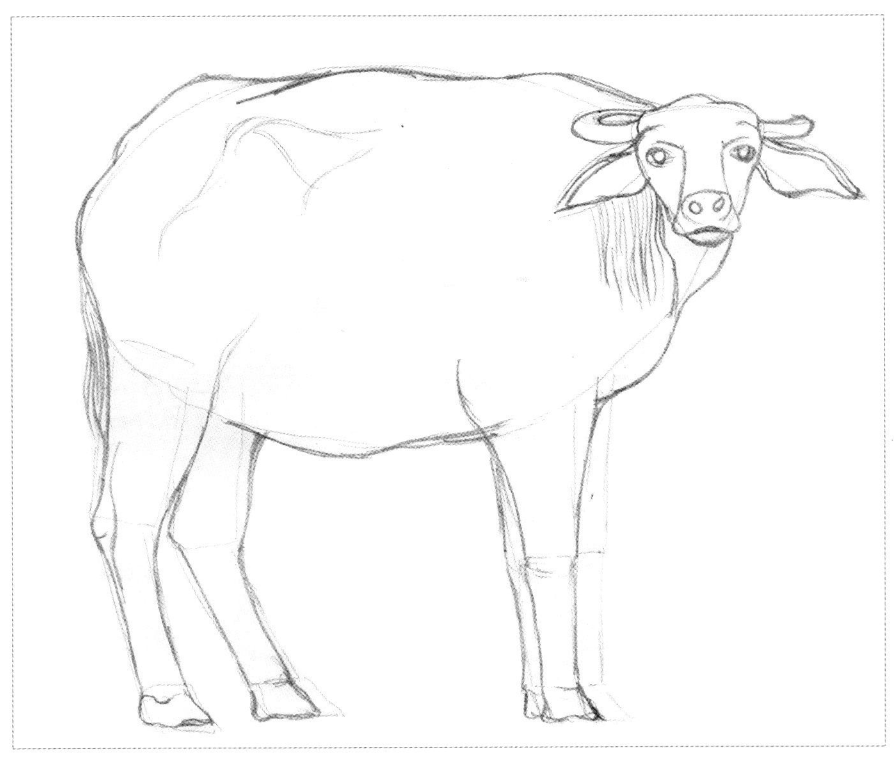

For the remainder of the session I asked the children to begin their own exploratory sketches of animals, keeping in mind what they had learnt that day. It was gratifying to see how they were increasingly confident about their ability to capture form. My modelling exercise had helped them understand that any complicated form could be pulled apart and broken down into simple lines and shapes.

"I'm going to try the rhinoceros because it is difficult."
Declared one child.
"But I think I can do it."

And he sat down to create his sketch, reference image in hand, breaking down the shape of the rhinoceros into simple, observable lines and shapes: an oval for the head, a larger oval for the body, and a series of rectangles for the legs.

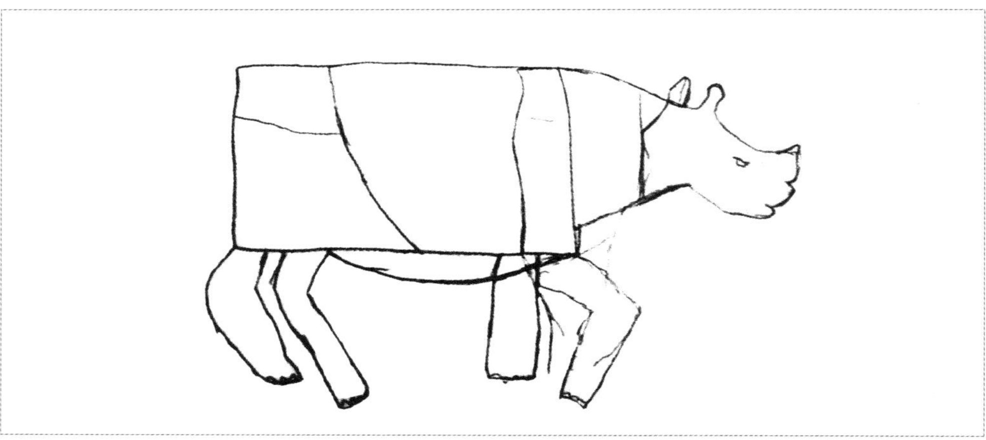

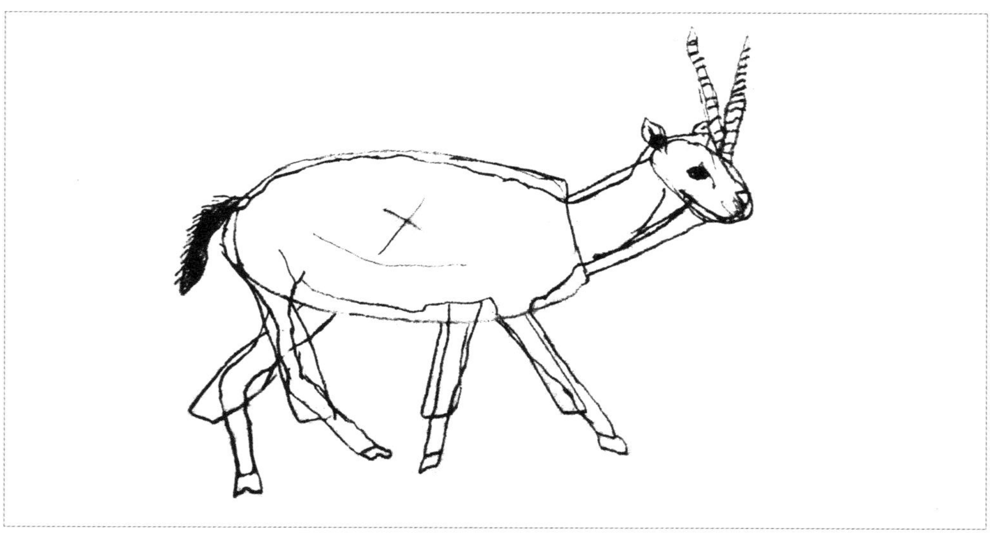

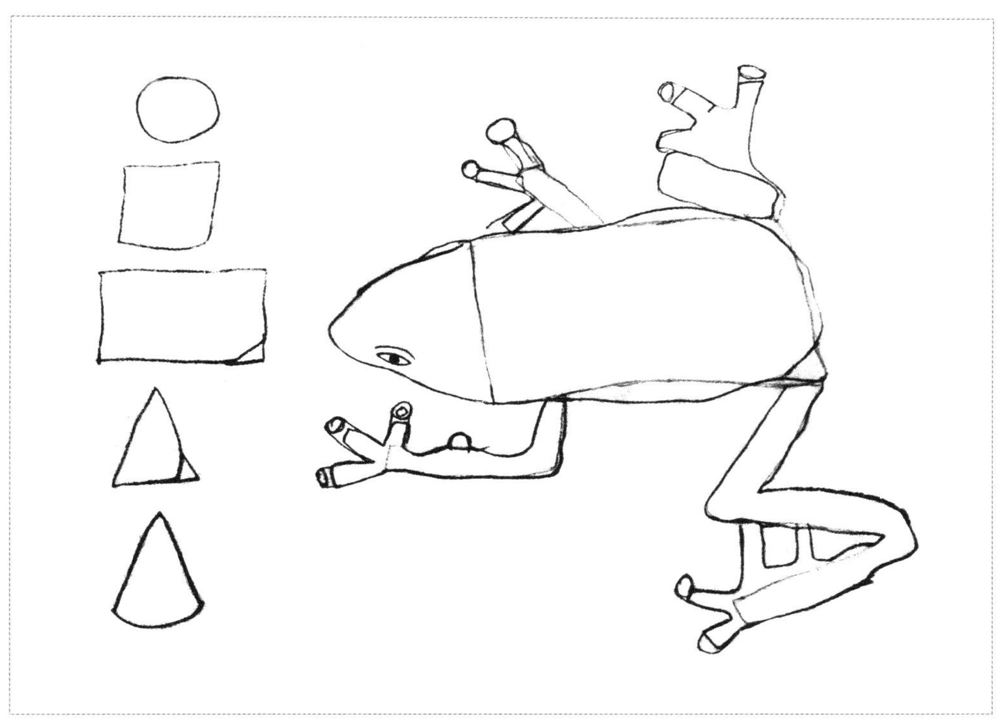

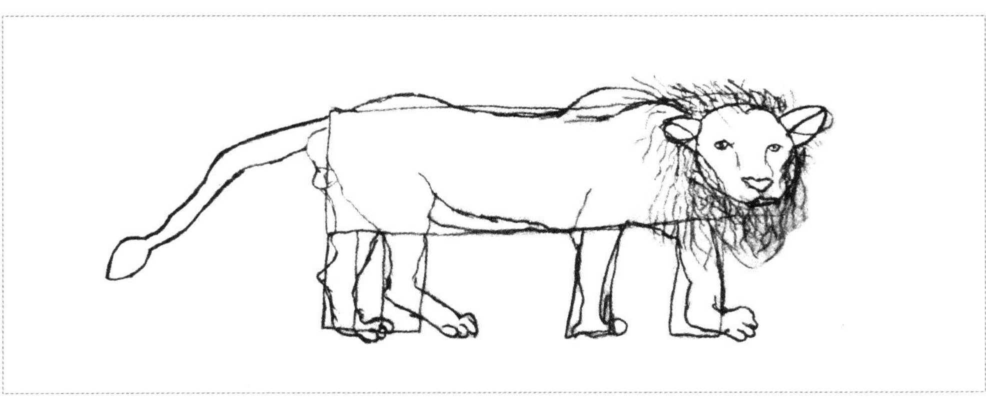

As an art teacher, when you pose questions to children, it's important to ensure that you stay open to all kinds of student responses, and resist the urge to tell them what you think is the 'right' one. But it's equally vital to lead your students to ground their responses in evidence. For instance, if you ask, "What shape is the buffalo's face?" and a child says, "Oval" instead of what you perceive is a triangle, ask the child to look closely at the image again and outline the observed oval shape with her finger. By doing so, the child can either support her own perception with evidence on why she thinks the face is an oval, or be free to change her mind. Other students can also be asked to join in the discussion, to show that there are multiple ways of seeing, responding and reasoning.

About Art

Children need to see drawing as something everyone, including themselves, are capable of doing. To gently guide them through their artistic development, it is good to evolve a set of practical methods and strategies that will demystify the drawing process for them. For example, encourage children to practice close looking. This helps them identify simple shapes embedded in complex forms. Once they start breaking down the mysteries of form thus, the drawing process becomes simpler, more accessible and less mysterious.

About the Learning Process

An instructional technique called "scaffolding" is a useful method which provides support for the learner, when they are introduced to concepts for the first time. It provides support, but shouldn't be misunderstood as handholding. It requires that you pull back slowly as children become more independent and self-directed in their learning.

Here are some examples of how you can use scaffolding in the classroom:

- Modelling: through demonstrations involve students actively, not only in the lesson goals you have planned, but also in your thinking process. In other words, think aloud as you demonstrate, and include the children's inputs as you go along.

- Linking: connect children's prior knowledge to the new concepts that you are introducing.

- Asking open-ended questions: encourage curiosity and reflection, which would also help you get a sense of how students are understanding what is going on. Pose such questions throughout class sessions, during demonstrations, while the children are working, and during discussions, when they get to reflect and critique what they have done.

When children copy stylised illustrations from the pages of a textbook or any other book, important decisions - how lines enclose a form, how forms are created, what details give us more clues about the image - are already made for them. Thus, they have almost no opportunity to sharpen their skills of observation, or make their own decisions about line and form. Neither do they get to explore a style of representation that could be uniquely theirs.

So I decided to focus my second session on observational drawing, using photos from the natural world. I wanted the children to look at the images closely, recognise subtle differences between them, and to think about what they observed. I wanted them to make thoughtful decisions about what to include and exclude in their drawing.

We began by looking at a set of images of diverse animals. I wanted the children to recall what they had learned in the previous class – about lines and shapes, and how any image can be broken down into simple shapes. I started with a photograph of a chameleon:

Here's a chameleon.
Can you look carefully at its different parts?
How is the head shaped?

13

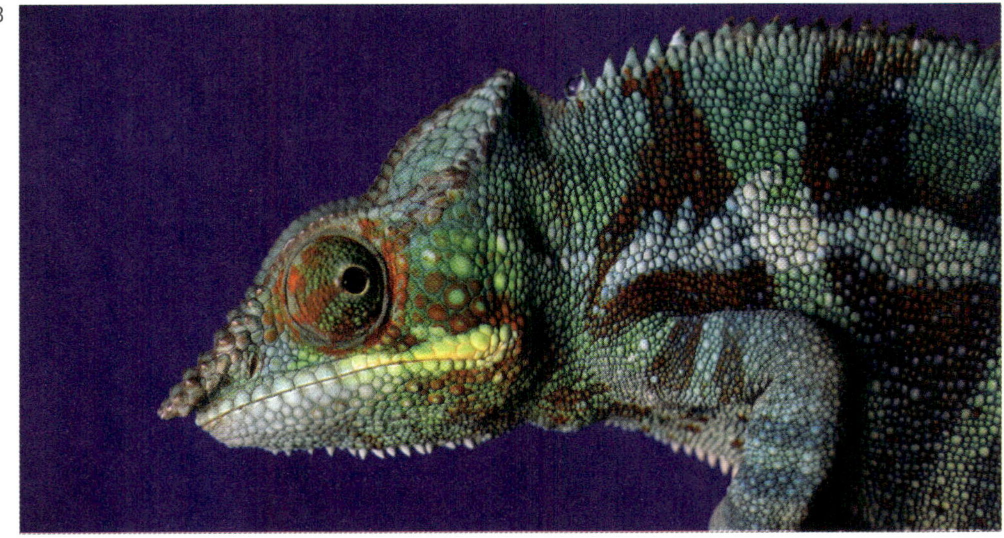

The children responded:

"[The] chameleon's head is a triangle shape."

"But it has [a] curve on top."

**What types of lines do you see
on the chameleon's head?**

"There is [a] zigzag line on the bottom
of chameleon's head."

How about the body? What shape is it?

"It's a semi-circle!"

"Top of [the] body is pointy."

And the tail?

"[The] tail has [a] line that is going in circles."

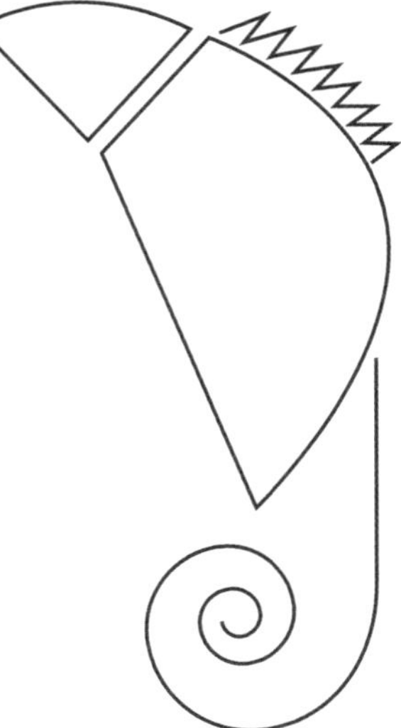

I now wanted the children to dig deeper into the visual information and to
introduce the concept of detail—something that gives more information:

**What else do you see when you look closely at the chameleon's head?
Let's look at the details... tiny things that tell us more. Is the eye a detail?**

"Yes!"

"[The] chameleon's head has many small bumps."

"No, not just small bumps. Some big, some small."

"...and some medium."

Why do you think the bumps are important details?

"Bumps will tell us skin is rough."

This thoughtful observation gave me the chance to introduce
the concept of texture as a detail—how something feels.

I could meanwhile see a spurt in their ability to observe, to look
closely and really see. They were not going by simple assumptions,
that is, given that most heads are round or oval, they didn't assume
that a chameleon's head is also oval. They had paid attention to actual
visible detail, to the fact that the chameleon's head was actually
more triangular in shape.

As the children responded to the questions posed, I started
on a simple sketch, lightly mapping out the lines and shapes that
they called out as they looked at the image of the chameleon.
Even as I sketched, I thought out aloud: I need to keep looking
closely at the photo...

I wanted children to keep their eyes focused on the photo
and extract visual information that I could include in my drawing.

"[The] nose is [a] small circle."

"No, it's [a] oval."

"[The] eye has many circles. Small circle, then big circles."

Once the preliminary sketch was done, I added these details,
using darker lines. I made sure that the children noticed which
of their suggestions I included and which ones I did not. I wanted
to show them how an artist trusts her eye, and includes some
details, but not others. My intention was to draw attention to
decision-making as an important part of art creation.

14 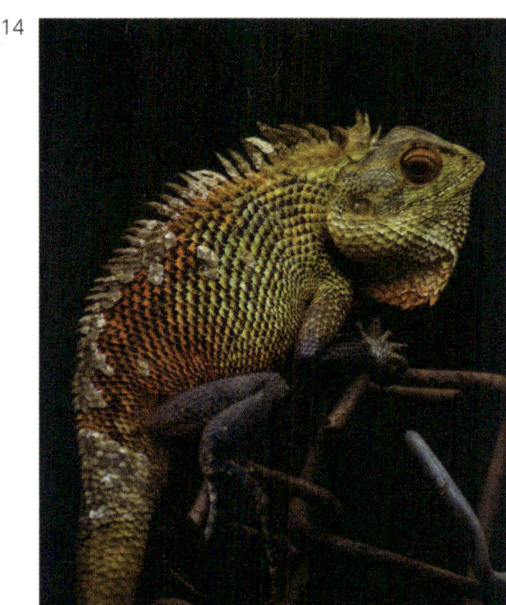

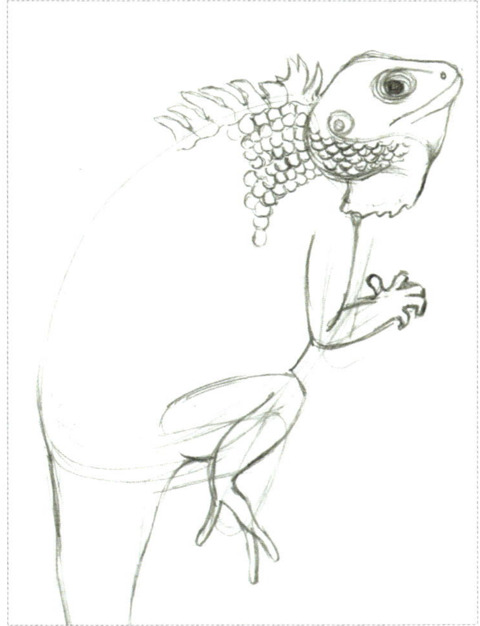

Once I was done with the drawing, the children began on
their own, choosing an animal from a range of images on hand.

What they came up with was astonishing. Quite evidently, their powers
of close observation had been honed. They were able to identify lines
and shapes in the reference photos, as well as capture details.

A child who took on the drawing of a tortoise, for instance, started
with a rough sketch, mapping the various shapes that she observed:
the shell was a semicircle, the head a small oval, the legs were rectangles.
She realised that the shell wasn't smooth, but made up of distinctive
mounds. She built beautifully on her preliminary sketch, using wavy
lines to render the undulations on the shell. Observing the markings
on the shell, she was able to use what she knew about geometric
and organic shapes to add this surface detail into her drawing.
She also noticed that the skin of the tortoise was rough, and chose
to depict this roughness using hatched lines as well as circular shapes
to depict the wart-like surface of the skin.

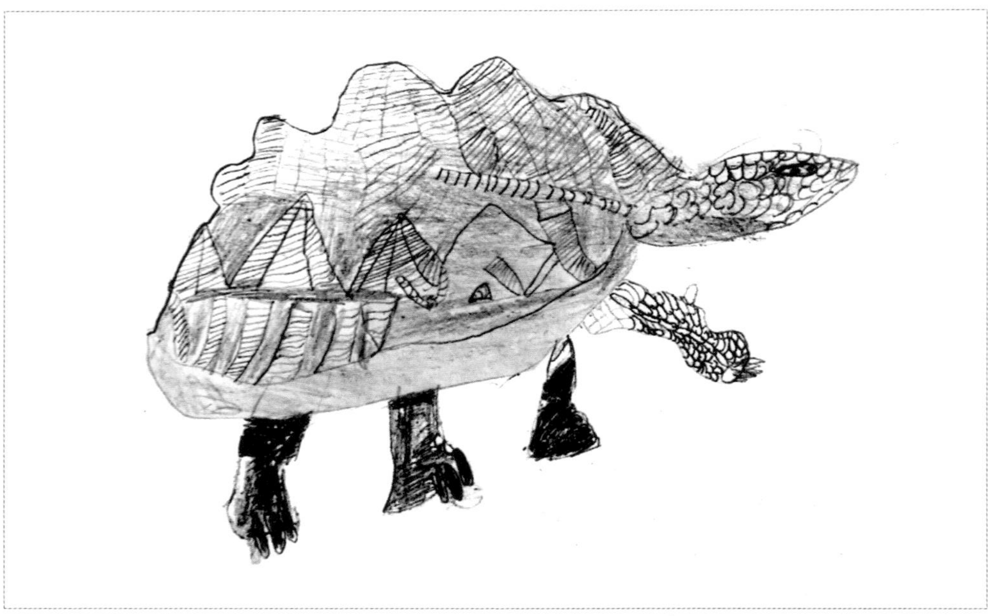

It's helpful to have a number of images to refer from—photocopied pictures will do.
Be sure to have a variety that children can choose from. Forming small groups
of 5 to 6 children, and distributing a bunch of images to each group gives children
the chance to choose which animal they'd like to draw. In the process, they also
learn to share image resources amongst each other.

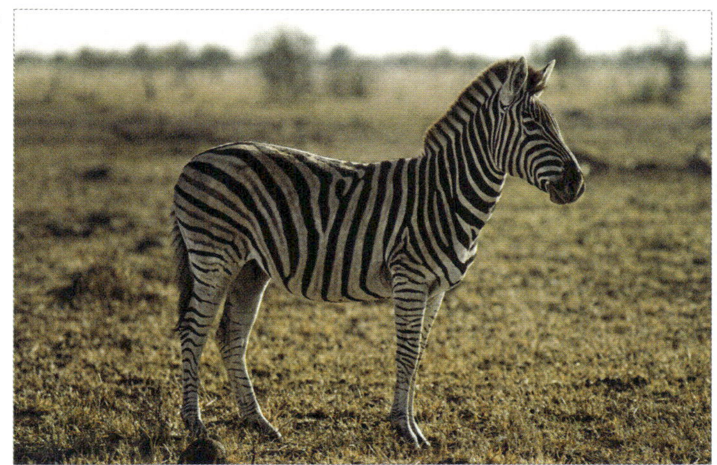

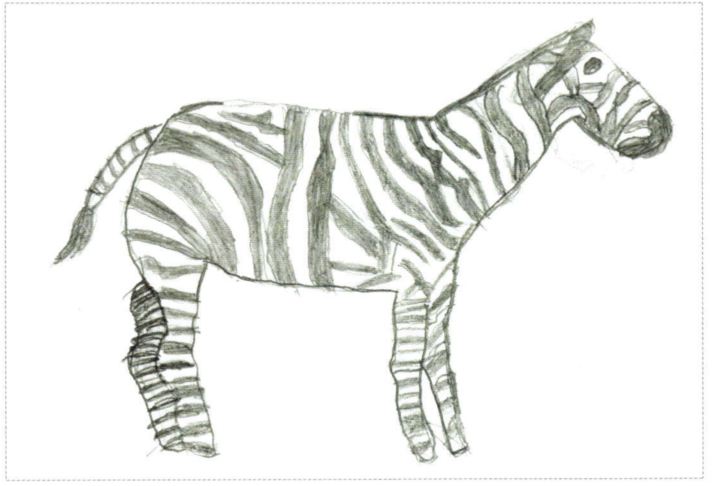

When children work on observational drawings, encourage them to create at least two different drawings. This helps them to practice and familiarise themselves with the process of breaking down complex forms into lines and shapes. If a child seems to need extra support, can't seem to get started on his own, or asks for help in drawing, resist the temptation to help him out by doing his work.

As a rule, never draw on a child's artwork. Help her move past her difficulties by utilising other strategies: re-engage her through conversation and guidance. If she has trouble capturing the animal form from a reference image, help her break it down into simple lines and shapes. Ask questions that would make her look closely, and enhance her observation skills. As the child responds, ask her to plot out the shape of the animal once more, with your guidance. Guide the child through this process actively, and provide her the one-on-one support she needs. At the same time encourage her to come up with her own solution.

When they had finished drawing one animal, I encouraged them to take on another. By repeating the experience, they could further refine their skills—of close observation, mapping shapes, looking at detail and making decisions on what to include. Creating art in this fashion was also a way to link better with their surroundings and to become more observant of what is around them, and what is within as well.

16

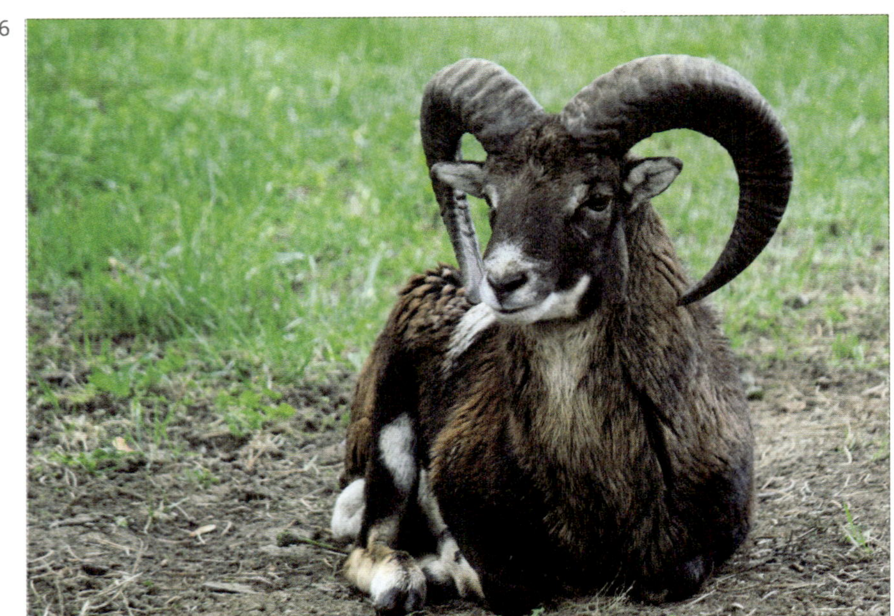

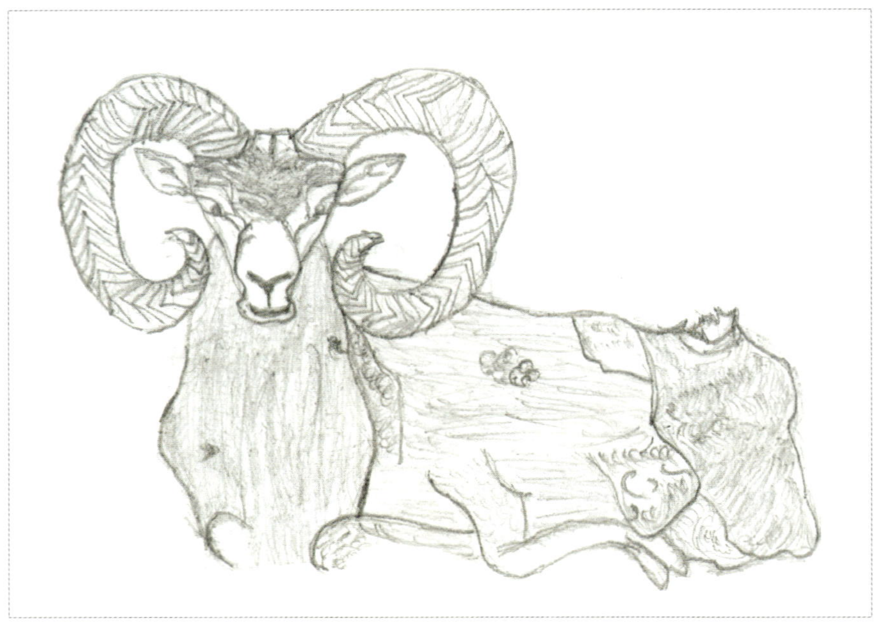

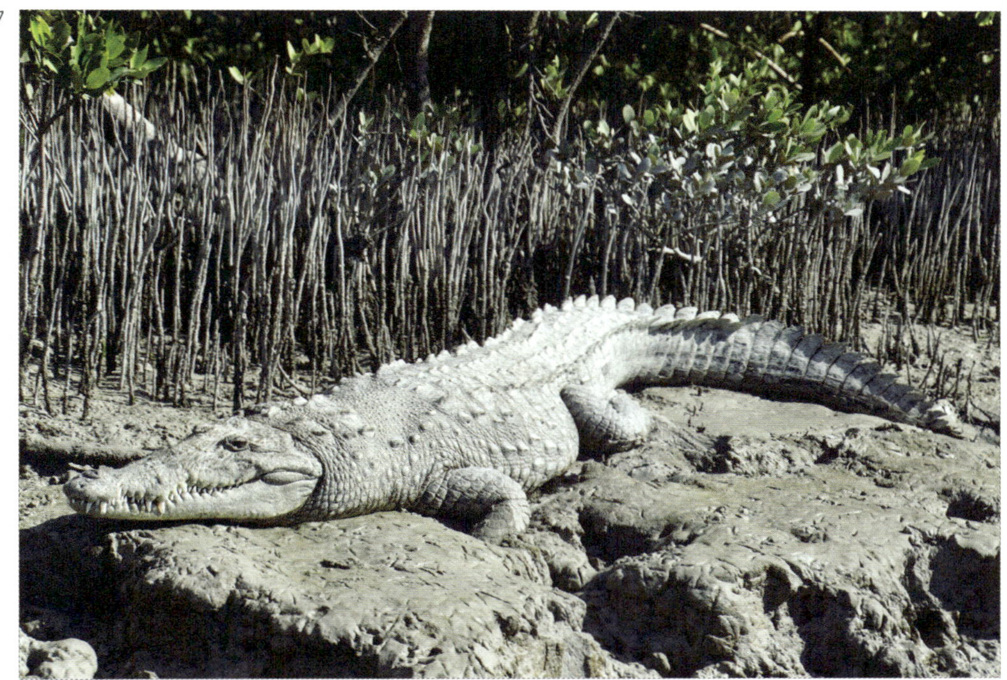

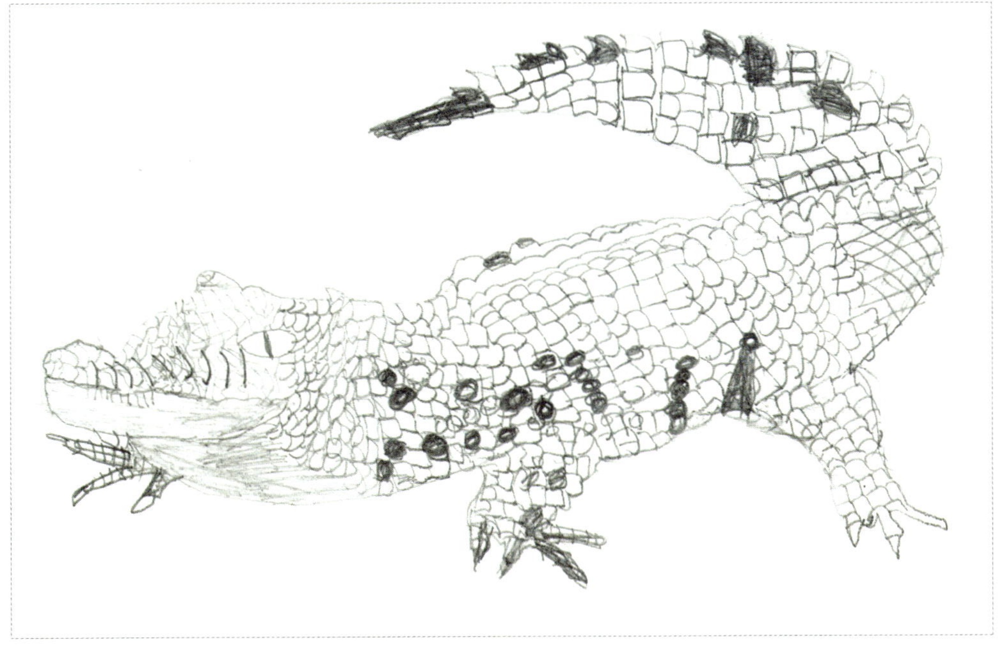

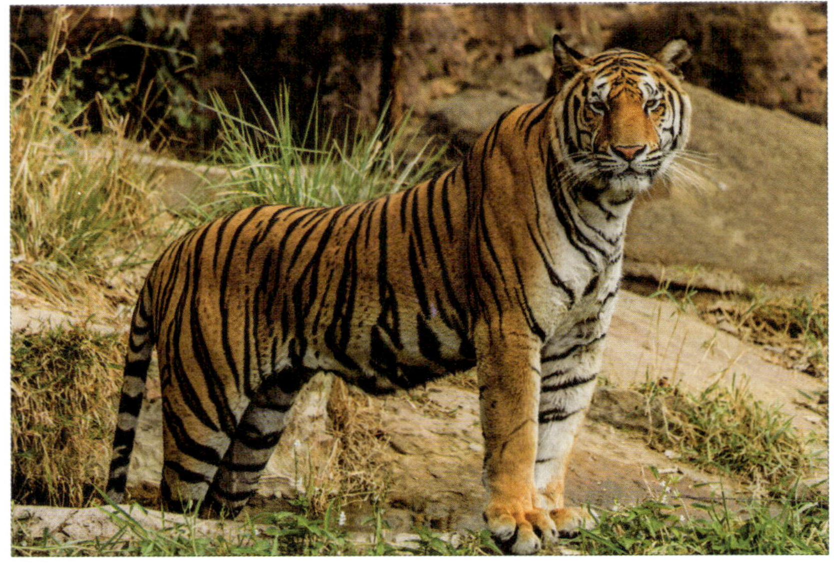

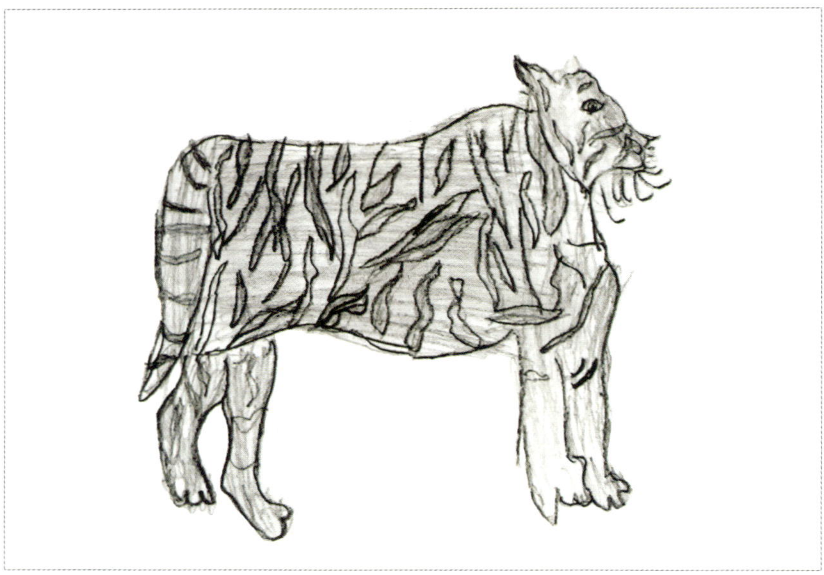

To be a good art teacher, you need to embrace the role of a coach and facilitator, rather than that of an instructor, who imparts concrete instructions that must be followed. So, instead of offering suggestions, it is more important to listen to students, affirm their ideas, and ask open-ended questions which help them think and make decisions on their own. Equally a teacher needs to spark students' imagination, boost their confidence and self-esteem, and help them manage frustrations that emerge when making art. The goal is to create a learning culture that enhances communication and collaboration, and at the same time upholds each child's uniqueness.

About Art

Being observant and paying close attention to detail is a valuable skill to possess—a skill which goes beyond the context of art-making. When you introduce observational drawing to children in a planned manner, they develop a capacity to work slowly and mindfully over time, and to train their eyes to really see. You can nurture this skill in other ways too: by continually giving them a chance to look at images closely; being ready to discuss and question what they're looking at; or giving them access to tools like a magnifying glass, through which they can look closely.

About the Learning Process

"Modelling" can be an effective pedagogical tool in the classroom—one that provides children with opportunities to observe the application of new concepts as they are introduced. There's a fine line however between modelling which expects students to merely follow what the teacher demonstrates and modelling that builds and scaffolds learning for children. The first approach stifles independent thinking and results in children mimicking what the teacher does. The second and more effective approach provides children with just enough support to enable them to take their learning forward on their own. It encourages them to ask questions and come up with their own solutions. This kind of pedagogy is different from the 'spontaneous' approach as well, which leaves children to do things on their own. Good modelling on the other hand actively guides children to get past what they know and to explore what they don't.

For your modelling to be effective, make sure all the children are actually actively engaged in the demonstration process. Think aloud when you're demonstrating, pose questions to students, enlist their support and guidance every step of the way, and invite student volunteers to assist you with your demonstration. All this will ensure that children take ownership of new ideas and concepts and explore them in their work.

Further, as a facilitator, it is important that you do the following: observe closely, explore, experiment, test out options, make thoughtful choices, persevere through difficulties, think flexibly, turn what could be 'mistakes' around... Modelling these behaviours consistently is bound to help children internalise these behaviours and make them their own.

FOSTERING IMAGINATION AND EXPRESSION

Imagine and Envision

Why is it important for children to envision what they wish to draw, before they sit down to do so?

Before we sit down to create anything original, we need to have, in our mind's eye, an image or at least a sense of what we wish to do. How do we develop this capacity to "see" before we draw, visualise or envision what is yet to be?

Artists do this in different ways. Some set a goal for themselves, and then plan each step that takes them closer to that goal. Others start with exploring materials: paint, oil pastels, collage paper and so on. Many start sketching. Howsoever they do it, most artists keep at what they have set out to do, until they arrive at a plan or have a clear vision of what they wish to create. An important part of envisioning is an artist's ability to think big. As their vision takes shape, they learn to step back and reflect on their work, and use their judgment to refine their ideas further.

Children as much as artists need to develop these abilities to envision, plan and reflect. This is particularly important in our educational context where they are used to only thinking of what is directly in front of them. The curricula and the textbook define their horizons and the opportunities to do something original are often limited. Art provides an excellent context for children to invent possibilities beyond their lessons and exams, and to visualise something new and work towards realising it.

Inventing Possibilities

To envision something original requires us to exercise our imagination. Imagination is the basis of all invention. And the art room is a tremendous space to nurture imagination. I devoted an entire session of my art classes to enable children to "imagine."

I began by showing them images of hybrid animals, mythical creatures, made up of a combination of one or more animals. The theme of imaginary hybrid animals was selected to help develop the children's imaginative capacities and enable them to think outside the box. The first image that I shared with them was a drawing of a creature that was part eagle, part horse. Giving the children a moment to observe the image closely, I asked them:

What animals have been combined in this picture?

They responded enthusiastically,
"Horse! Eagle!"

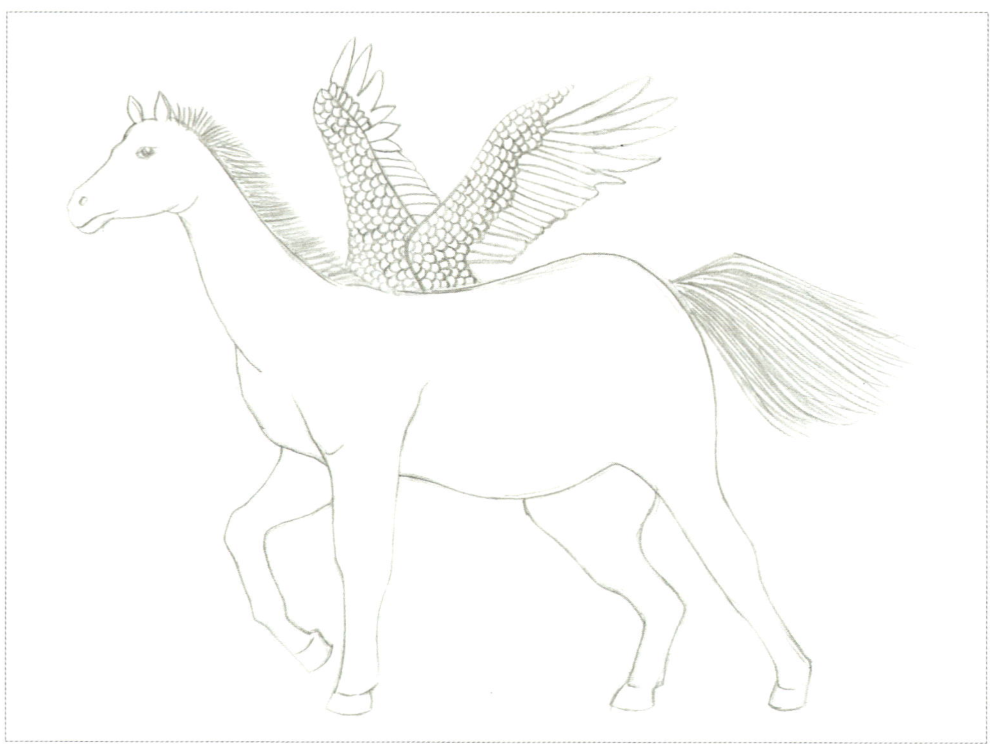

Wanting the children to construct their own interpretations
of what they were looking at, I said:

Describe an eagle. What kind of personality does an eagle have?

Swift responses followed:

"[An] eagle has big wings."

"[An] eagle can fly."

"[An] eagle is strong."

I moved on to the horse. And they responded as before.

"[A] horse is beautiful."

Another child cut in,

"It runs fast."

And a third said, rather unexpectedly,

"A horse is very kind."

I followed up with questions that would jog their minds,
and stretch their imagination.

Where do you think this hybrid animal lives?

"Forest!"

A group of children chorused.

Wanting more responses, I asked:

Who has a different idea?

"[The] horse ... will live in [the] village."
observed a thoughtful child.

What special powers do you think this hybrid animal has?

"The horse and eagle animal is the king of a forest. He is very beautiful
and strong. He will use the eagle wings to fly up to the sky. From up he
will be seeing all the forest and he will be protecting the forest."

Another child - who had earlier noted that the horse was
a kind animal - proclaimed:

"When [the] horse is angry it will change to [the] eagle."

The children's responses were mostly descriptive, yet not uniform.
Some had called attention to the characteristic traits of an eagle and
a horse, while others were more imaginative and interpretive.

I pointed out to the children that they had heard varied interpretations of the same picture—which meant that different people can see the same thing differently.

I continued with the exercise, showing the children a few additional images of hybrid animals.

I wanted them to pay attention to how different artists had combined two animals into one, and to notice the thoughtful choices made in each instance. Pointing to one such picture, a child noted:

"Elephant head [is] put on bird body."

I asked,

Could these two animals be combined differently?

"Put birds' wings on elephant body."

"Add bird legs to elephant body."

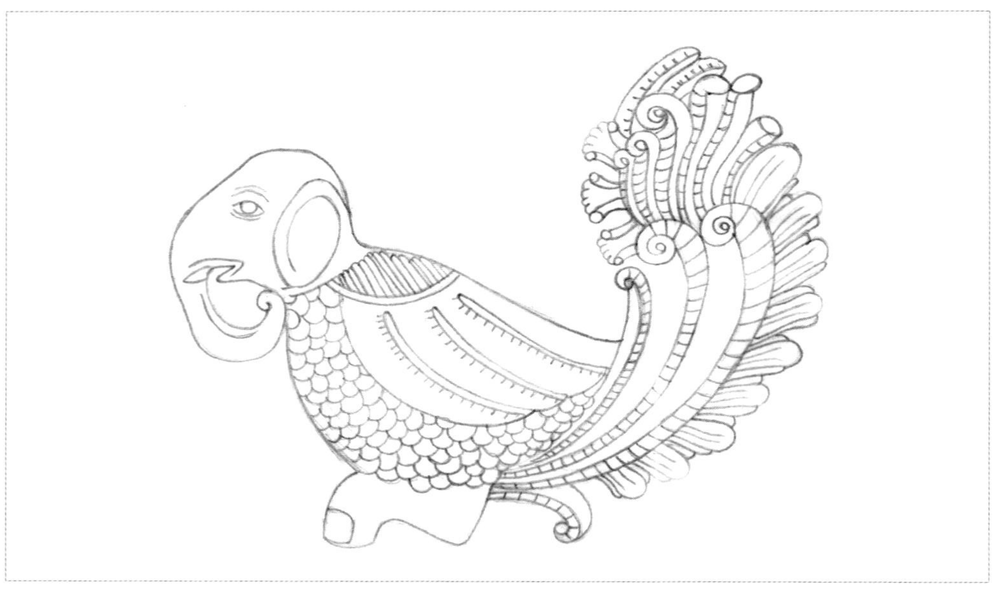

Before you start an activity, it is useful to brainstorm with the children and encourage them to come up with multiple solutions. Brainstorming helps jumpstart the imagination and ensures that children have more than one idea to work with. It is also important to be strategic about images that you hand out—for example, make sure that you don't include the images used by the teacher during her modelling session. Also, encourage children to envision and work out solutions on their own, rather than recreate what the teacher had done.

The children had begun to notice that an artist can choose from several alternatives before him, and by remaining open to various possibilities, he could exercise his imagination freely. Wanting the children to have yet another opportunity of seeing how animals might be inventively combined, I brought out the reference photographs of animals I had shared with them earlier, and said:

Choose 3 animals.
Let me try and combine their features to make a new animal.

The children recommended that I work with pictures of a camel, elephant, and eagle. I began to sketch, modelling the thoughtful decision-making that goes into creating something new and unexpected. Eventually, I came up with a creature that had a camel's head, neck, body, and legs, elephant's trunk, and an eagle's wings.

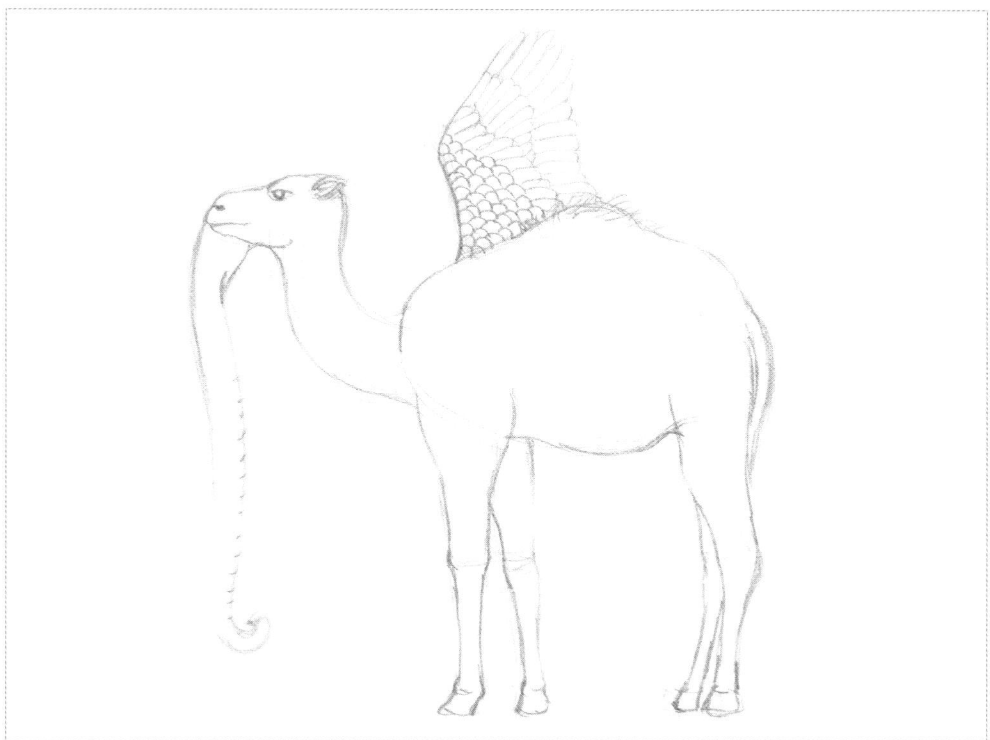

Your turn now,
I said, turning to the children,
You tell me how you would combine these animals,
and I will sketch, as you speak.

Asked to come up with additional and alternative solutions, the children offered several suggestions. One such example was to combine the camel head and neck with the elephant body and legs, while using the eagle wing to form the tail.

I then asked the children to go through the animal reference images and select a few to work with. The children were excited:

"I am going to put together a deer and a turtle—the deer will have a turtle shell for its back!"

"My animals will have a cheetah's head and a rooster's body."

I announced that each child would need to sketch at least two different hybrid animals. This would help them explore different ways of combining animals and also to pick on the options that worked best for them.

As the children got to work, I moved around the room, and engaged them in one-on-one discussions. I asked each child why she or he had chosen to work with a particular set of animals: Had they considered the individual characteristic traits of the animals they were combining? Did they have specific reasons for wanting to combine these animals? My questions were meant to make them pause and consider their choices and reflect on them, so that they could thoughtfully construct their hybrid animal characters.

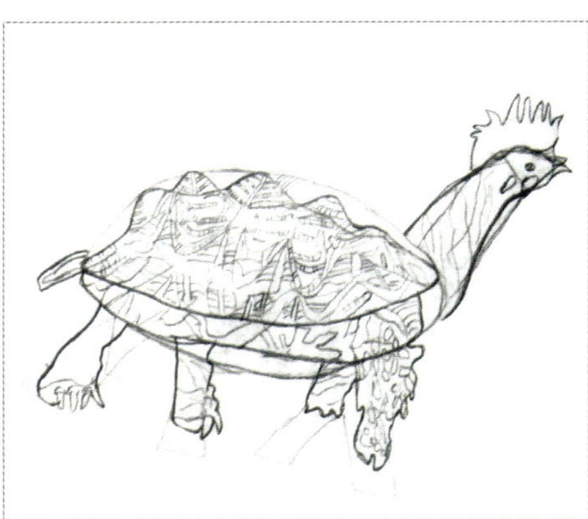

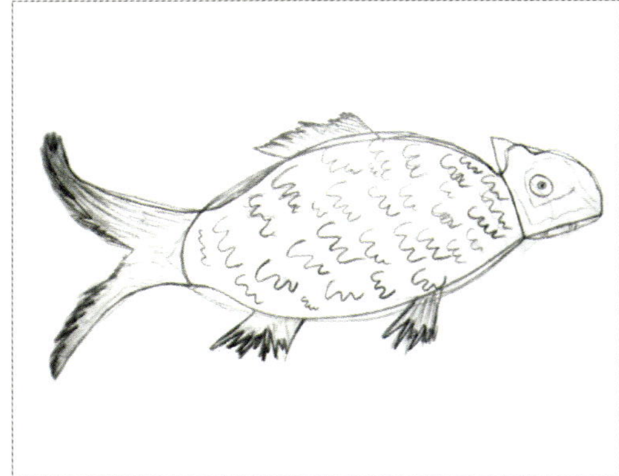

Children sometimes tend to copy from each other, or from the pictures of hybrid animals already shown to them. It is important therefore to be clear about your expectations, as far as this exercise is concerned. Be clear that you would like them to test out a few combinations themselves and come up with their own unique solution. This helps minimise the chances of copying.

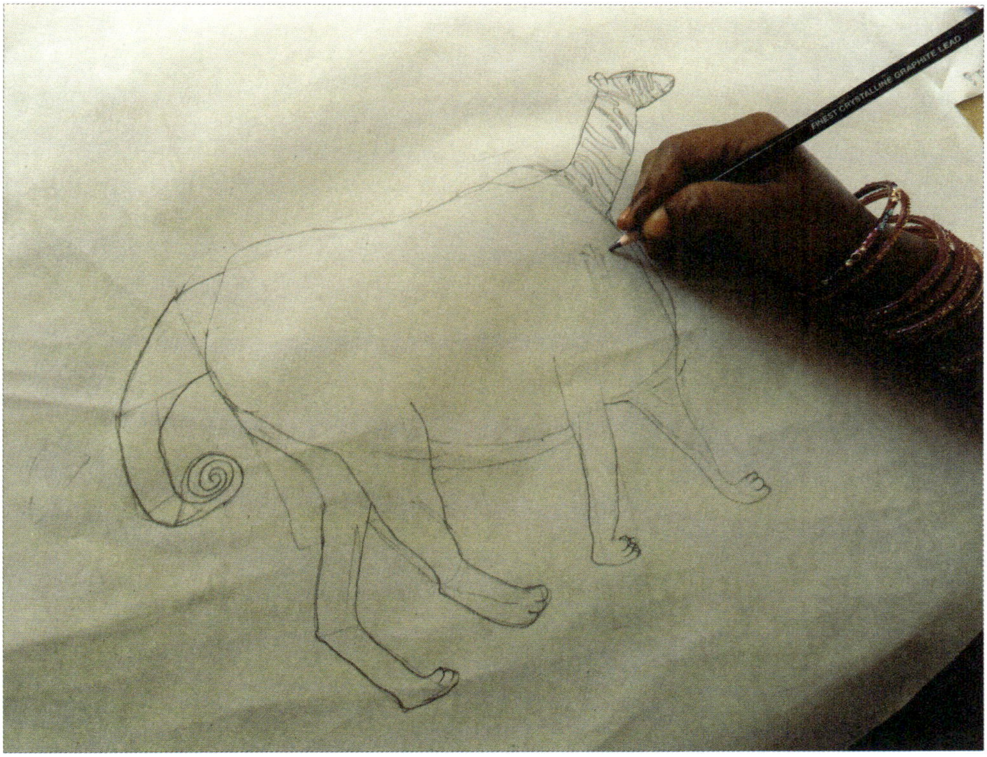

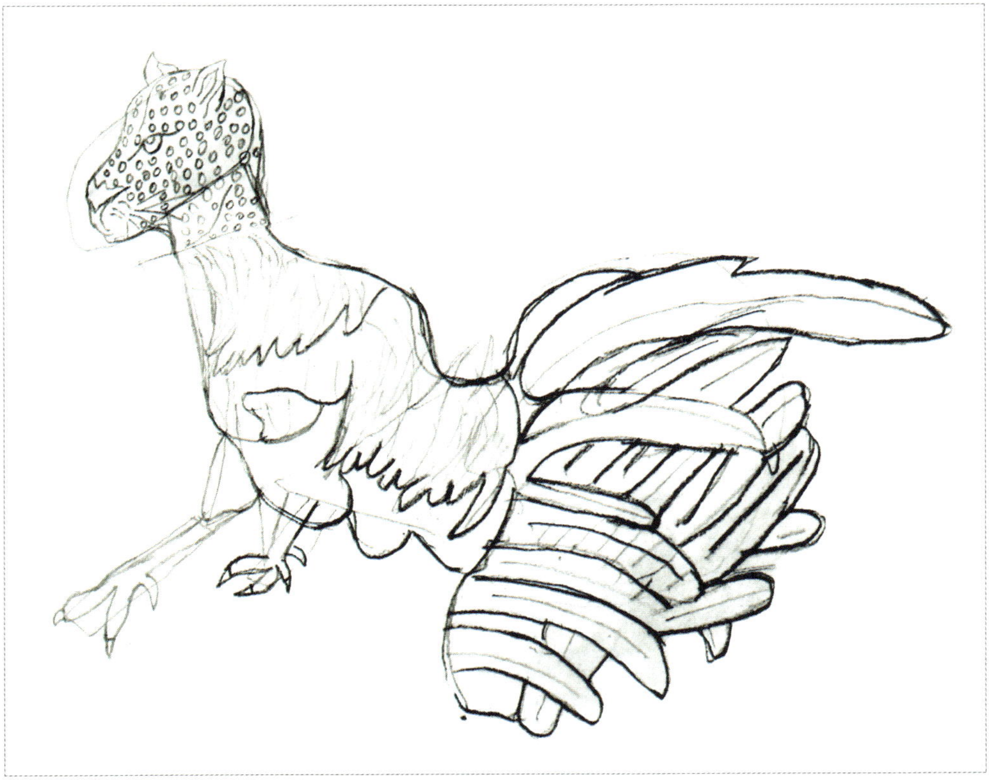

FINEST CRYSTALLINE GRAPHITE LEAD

Watching the children draw, I realised that they possessed an immense capacity to come up with not just one, but two (and in some instances three or more) unique and thoughtfully constructed solutions. One child, for example combined a tiger's head, turtle's body, and chameleon's tail. She went on to explain her choice thus: this animal can not only hide in its shell but also blend into its environment, and so had the power to surprise an unsuspecting hunter with its ferociousness.

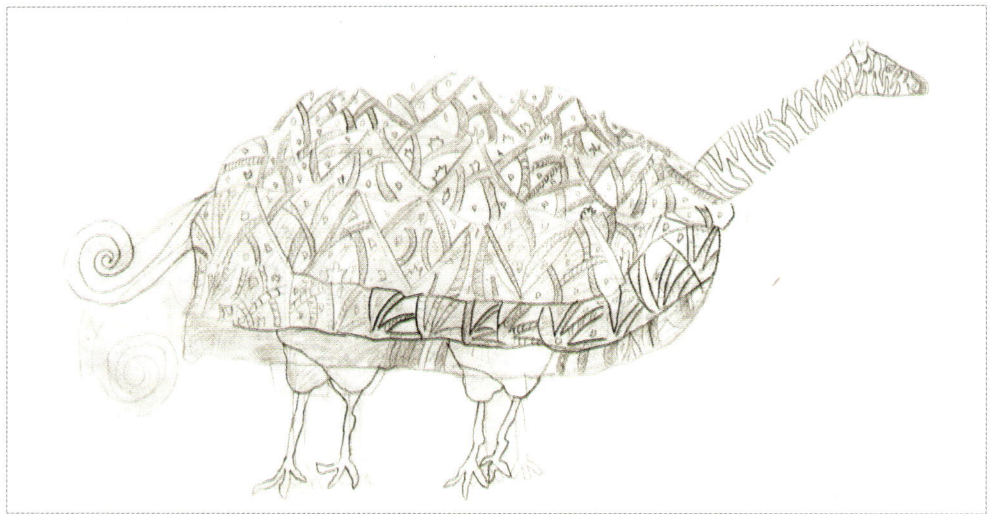

Once all children had thought through and sketched their animal combinations, I asked them to pick their favourite solution for their hybrid animal character. I suggested that they go on to create a detailed enlarged drawing of the same and modify their work in whatever manner they considered necessary. They were to work on and use the entire sheet of paper. I wanted them to learn the process of "scaling up" a drawing.

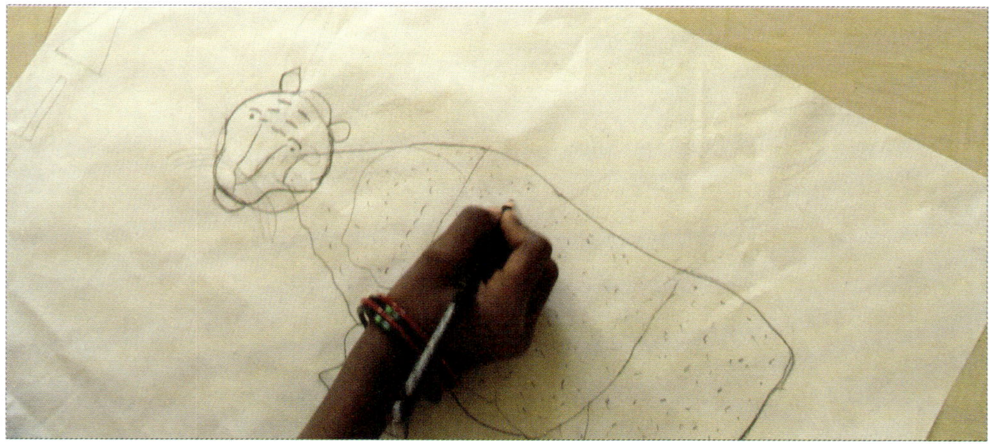

About Art

An artist's practice is an imaginative undertaking. But great ideas
do not occur in a vacuum. Artists investigate to see what else exists and
set themselves challenges. They play with materials, and continuously push
the boundaries of their creative thinking to come up with something original.
Tools such as brainstorming and exploring multiple options to solve an artistic
problem help them identify creative possibilities, of which they were not
aware earlier. Ideally, an art classroom ought to provide children with similar
opportunities—to immerse themselves in the art process, exercise their
imaginative capacities, and develop their own unique solutions.

About the Learning Process

Schools in India, and society in general, think in two contradictory ways
about creativity in art. On the one hand, they label anything that results from
an art activity 'creative'—it does not matter if the child has merely followed
a template and her work lacks original thought. On the other hand, creativity
is linked to 'talent'. Ironically this is narrowly defined, as the capacity to capture
likeness, whether in drawing, painting, or any other artistic medium. Creativity
is also often construed as the outcome of a muse that only some possess.

However, as my exercises with 6th standard students show, children's
creativity does not have to do only with what we consider skill and talent.
Neither does it have to do with an mysterious impulse or inspiration alone.
Children develop creativity as a result of unfettered exploration. I started off
with sessions in which my students explored form and shape through drawing.
I followed these up with extended moments of idea generation, reflection,
critique, and refinement. As these sessions unfolded, I could see how, literally,
children grew increasingly 'creative.' As they worked, they displayed a growing
capacity to make choices about what to draw, follow through on ideas, stay
with certain thinking processes and finally connect what they imagined with
what they did.

In order to foster creative imaginative thinking in the art classroom,
in all its richness, it is essential to redefine and broaden our notions
of creativity. It is necessary to view creativity, not as a product but as
an artistic process involving inquiry, exploration, idea generation,
imagination and innovation.

 # Building a Puppet

After the children had created detailed drawings of their unique imaginary hybrid animals, they used their drawings as models to build puppets. The process involved was elaborate and unfolded over 6 sessions. It gave students from the 6th standard a unique art-making experience, and one that they had not engaged with before.

I started the first of these 6 sessions with a question:

Who has seen a puppet before?

All hands shot up in the air.

What types of puppets have you seen?

"Gombeyatta puppets!"

"Hand puppets!"

"You show[ed] us [shadow] puppets."

My next question was:

What do you think puppets are used for?

"To tell stories, like [from the] Mahabharata."

"Puppets [also] give message[s] about problems in [the] community,"
Said a child.

"About dowry…"
Another added.

"[About the] importance of reading and writing."

I showed them two images of puppets, one a shadow puppet and other a hand puppet, and I encouraged the children to comment on their differences.

"[Shadow] puppet is flat!"

"We see shadow puppet from front only."

"[Hand] puppet is round. [It is] not flat."

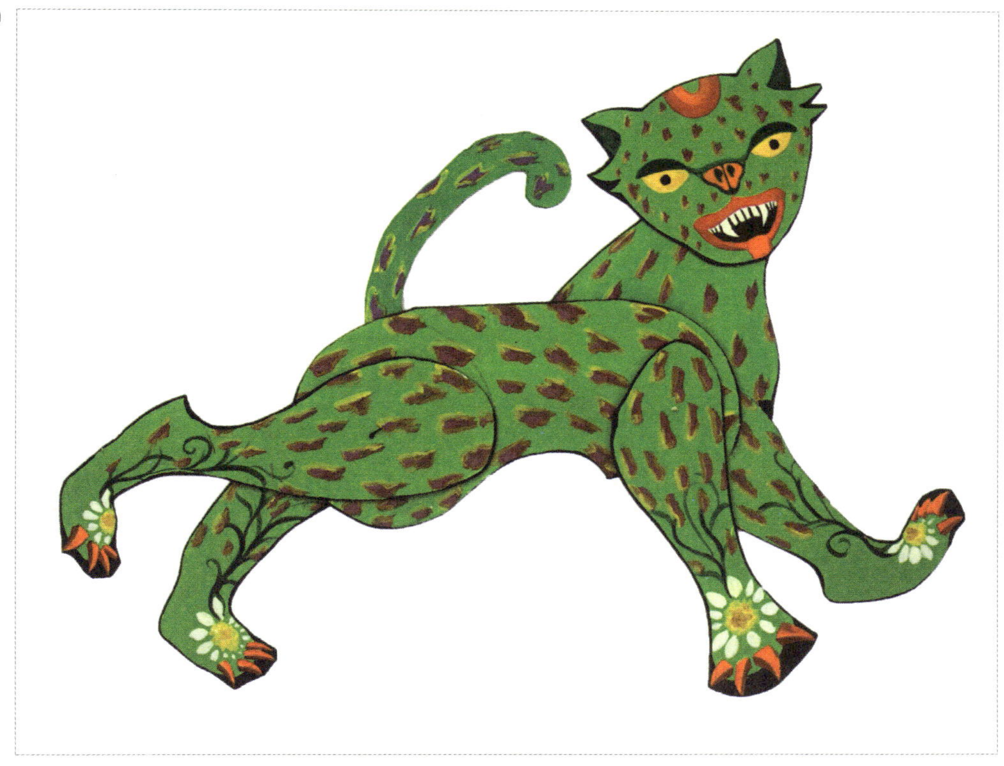

19

20

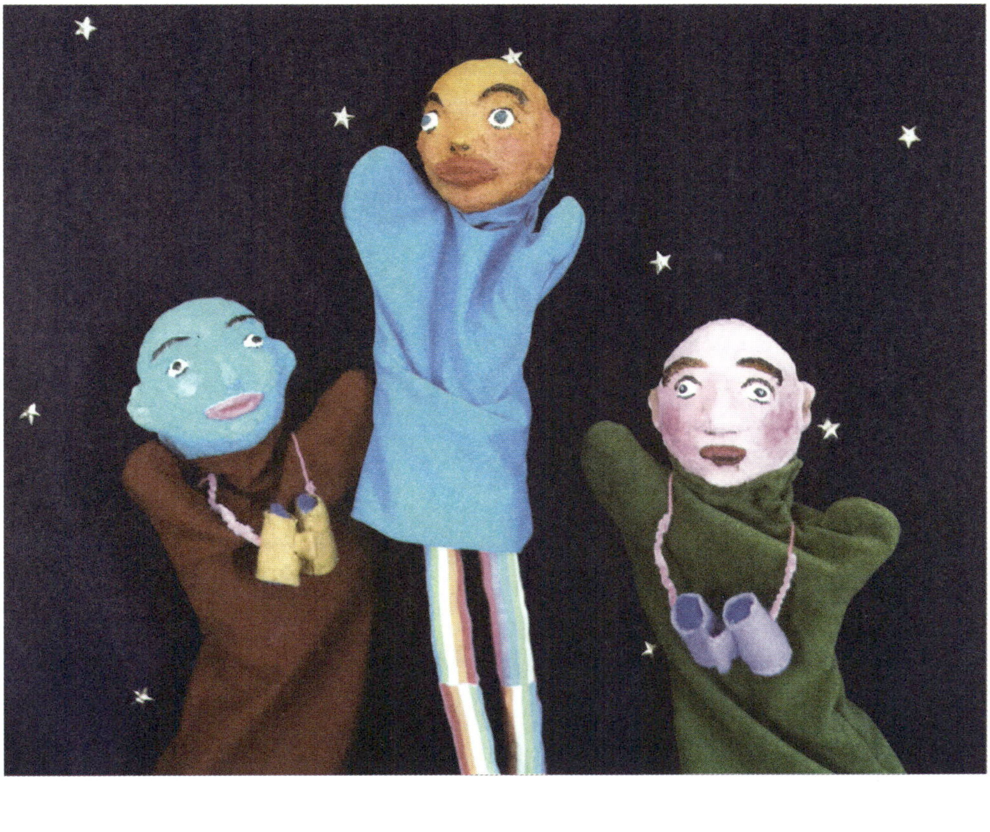

I wanted them to observe even more keenly. So I said:

How else are these puppets different?
Take your time, observe carefully before you answer.

"[Shadow] puppet is using paper. [Hand] puppet is using clothes to make."

An observant child noted:
"[The] hand puppet is moving with hand.
[The] shadow puppet is using the sticks."

Once the children were clear about the differences, I moved on to the task I was going to set them: the making of a shadow puppet. I returned to the images I had and pulled out one of a shadow puppet. I asked the children:

What are some important things that the artist had to
think about when he or she made this shadow puppet?
For example, what size is the puppet?

The children carefully considered my questions and responded,
"[The] puppet is big."

"[The artist is] thinking how to make [the] puppet big."

21
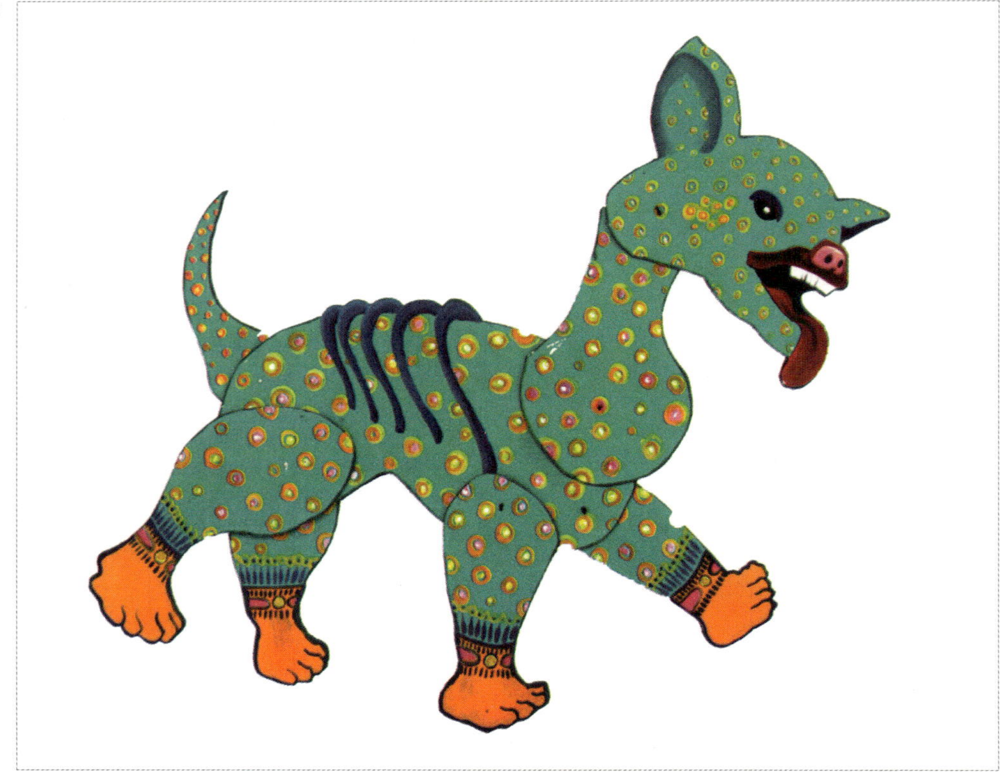

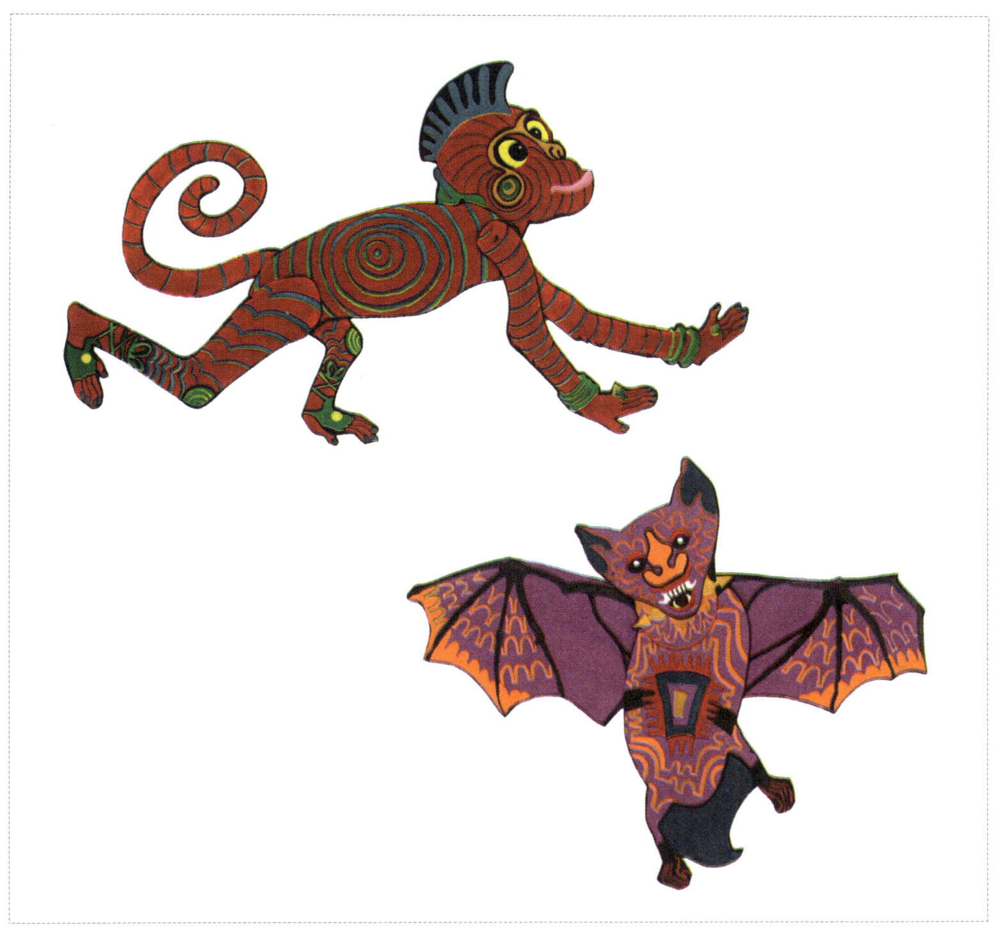

22

Wanting the children to think about the relationship between various aspects of the puppet and the shadows it causes, I continued:

Is the puppet simple and plain?

"No! It has many designs."

Look closely. What do you notice about the designs?

"[The] design are cut out."

Notice the shadow. Describe what you see.

"It has beautiful designs."

When you look at the shadow, do you see the front of the animal's face, or side view? What do you see?

"Side view."

"I can see nose, mouth, chin."

As in earlier sessions, I modelled the art-making process for the children. I referenced the imaginary hybrid animal drawing I had created in the previous session. I asked the children to use their close observation skills to help me identify the lines and shapes that made up the torso of my hybrid animal.

With the children's suggestions in hand, I started by drawing the animal's torso, because it helps set the size of the puppet. Since all other parts, the head, neck, and limbs all emerge from the torso, these could be developed in relationship to it. I drew on to thick black construction paper (chart paper) using a white drawing pencil.

I used the entire sheet, edge-to-edge, to draw out the torso form. The children had previously learned to scale up an image, and I wanted to re-emphasise the importance of scaling. Once the torso of the animal was completed, I enlisted the children's help to identify and add select surface details.

After the initial discussion and demonstration, I asked the children to start work on their puppets. Like I had done, they too would use their own hybrid animal drawings as a reference while creating their puppets out of the thick black construction paper.

The children started with the torso and spent an entire session drawing the body of their puppets.

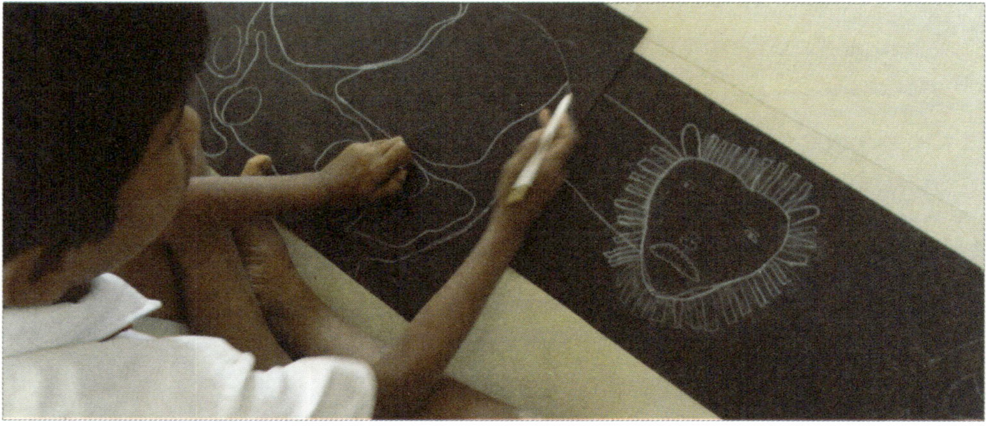

As the children work on the various parts of their puppets, encourage them to think about size relationships—between the head and the body, and between the head and body on the one hand, and limbs of the animal, on the other. This will help them understand the important concept of proportion.

As the children drew, I went around the class, and sat with each of the students. I suggested that they observe their sample drawing carefully, so that they could add visually interesting surface details to their puppets torso, for example, details to depict hair, scales, and other surface textures.

Once they had finished with the torso, the children developed the head and neck of their puppets in the following session, and the limbs of their hybrid animals in the third. Participatory demonstrations that involved modelling, conducted at each stage, enabled the children to understand how to create these various parts in relation to their animals' torsos.

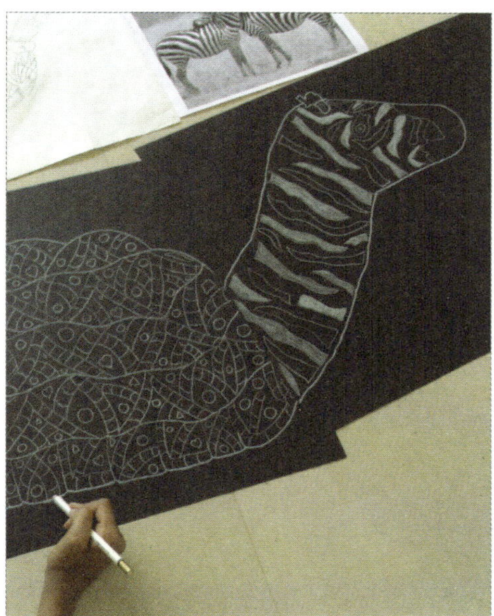
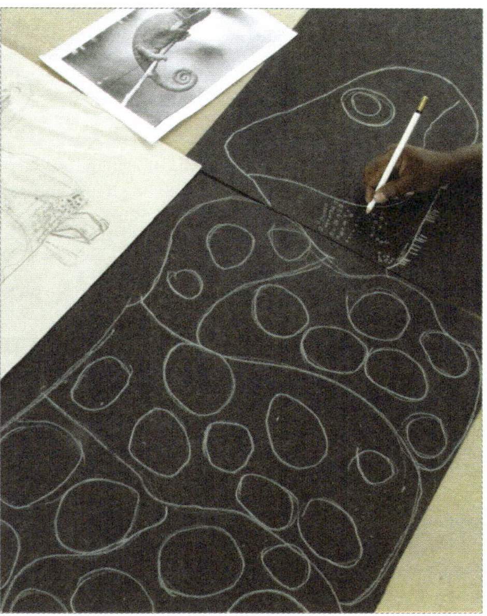
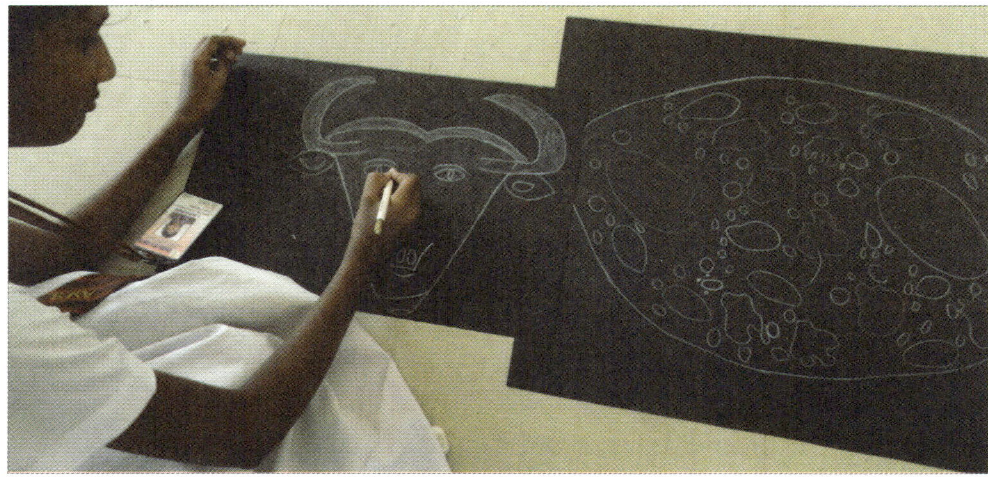

Once all parts were completed, I took the children through the process
of cutting up their drawings into their various component parts: head,
body, limbs and also the smaller and more delicate surface details.
I used my sample puppet to demonstrate cutting. And, since cutting
requires practice, I also encouraged the children to investigate using their
scissors in different ways to cut into the details that were drawn onto
spare sheets of construction paper.

It was not easy to cut into the thick construction sheets. But as
they continued to practice, they got better at it. After practicing,
they got to their hybrid animal parts and began to cut them up
carefully, including the delicate surface patterns.

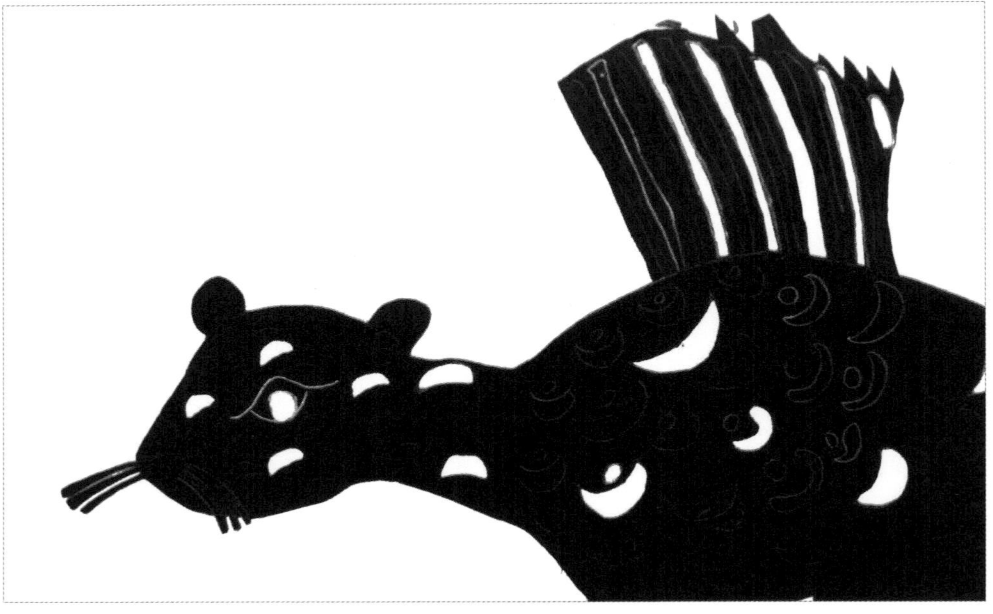

Provide children opportunities to get comfortable with cutting. Some children
might need more time than others, especially when it comes to cutting the surface
details. Giving children spare pieces of construction paper with the details drawn can
help them practice cutting. As they explore cutting, children have the opportunity
to discover for themselves some best practices. For example, using the tip of a scissor
to gently pierce into the black construction paper, and the center of a detail, to aid
the cutting out of that detail. Children also have the opportunity to identify common
pitfalls encountered while cutting, and offer solutions to the group to help avoid them
in the future. For example, cutting details that are too close to each other, and thereby
inadvertently cutting out an unintended chunk of the paper.

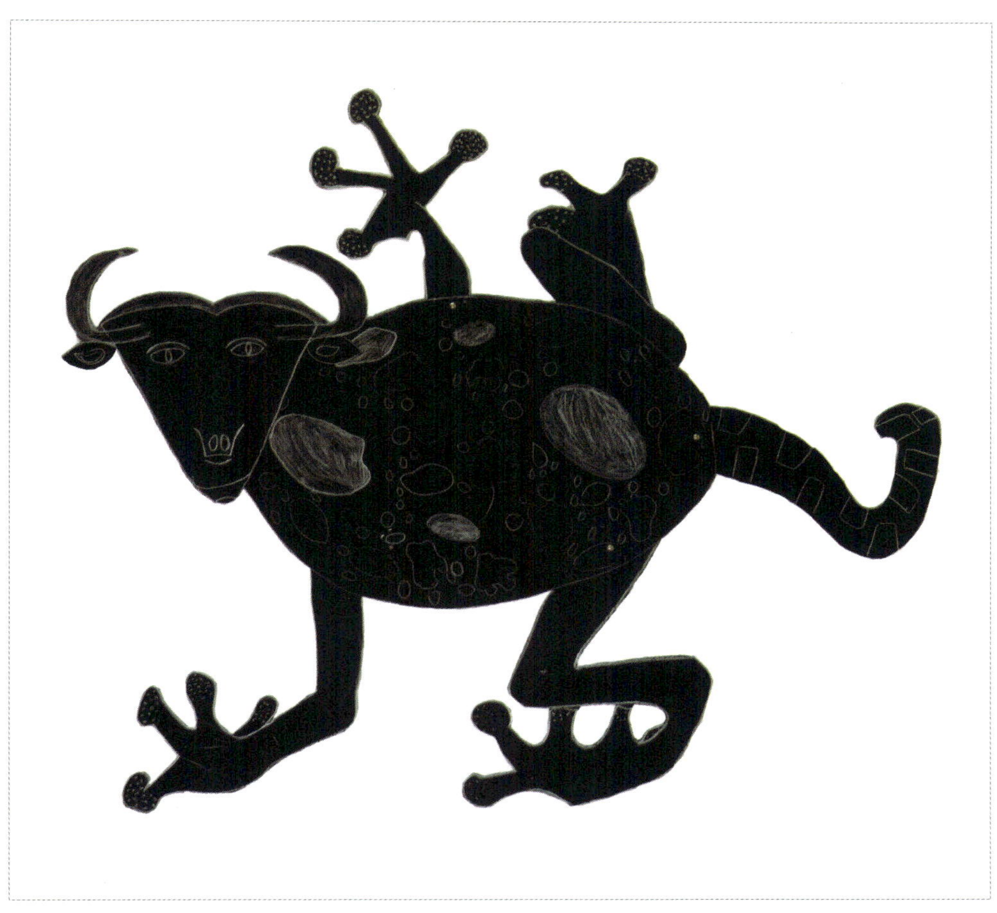

The next thing to be done was to put the different parts of the hybrid animal puppets together. But before they did that, the children had to decide which parts of their animal would move, and which parts wouldn't. I asked the children:

Pick a maximum of two parts of your hybrid animal that will move.

I explained to them that picking more than two parts would make it difficult for them to both hold their puppets and move the select parts.

"I will make legs move,"
A child responded.

"My animal head is moving when [it is] talking,"
Said another.

"I will show head and tail moving so I can hold [my] puppet,"
Said a third.

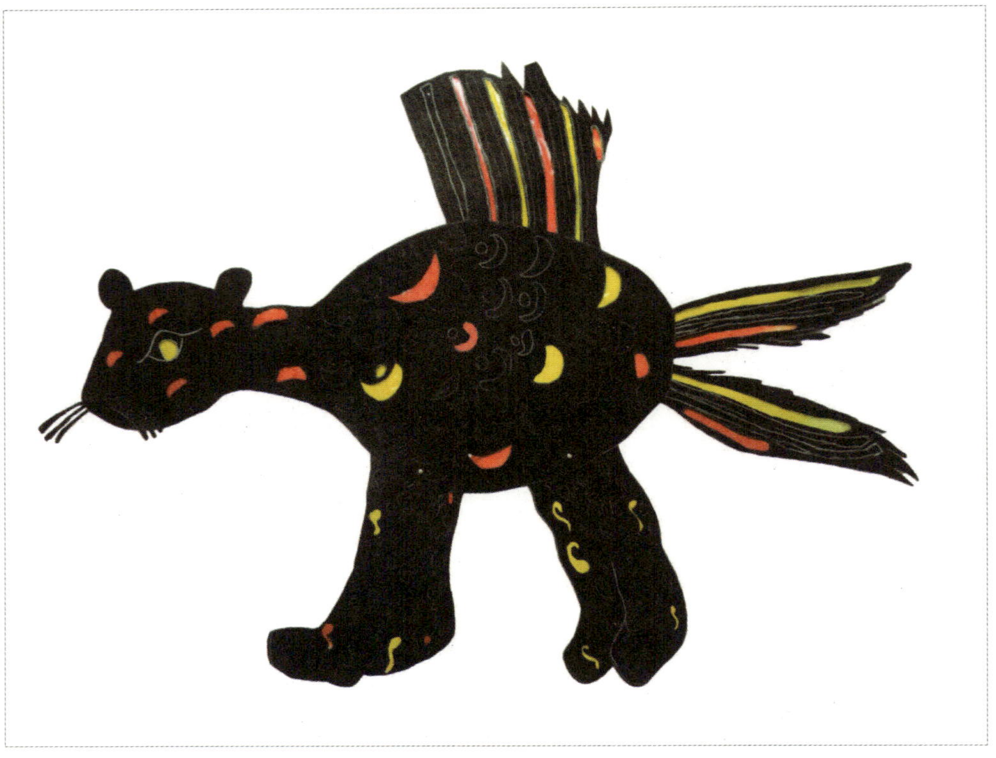

Once these decisions were made, we went onto the next stage.
Brads were introduced to the children as a way to create moving parts,
and glue to affix immovable parts. Once this was done, I suggested to
the children that they could decorate their puppets if they liked—such
as adding small swatches of coloured cellophane to select cutout details.
While some chose to add the cellophane in order to bring an element
of colour into their puppets, others chose not to use the cellophane.
They preferred the simplicity of using the white pencil, drawn out
patterns, and strategically cutout details.

As they held their puppets up, the children began to realise that they
were flopping over. A discussion about reinforcing their puppets ensued.
I introduced ice-cream sticks to the children. And we discussed how they
could be placed strategically on the back of the puppets to strengthen
the puppets and give them a certain rigidity. Following this discussion,
children were paired up and asked to support one another as they
collectively figured out where to affix the popsicle sticks to give their
puppets the necessary support and reinforcement.

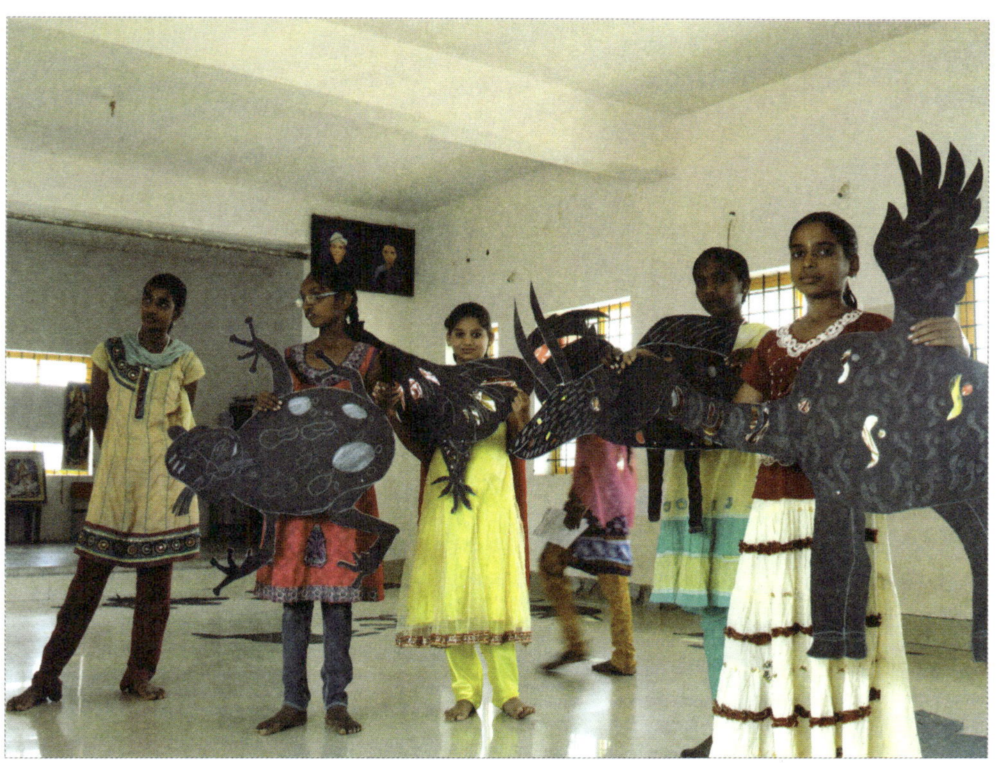

As the children worked on their puppets over 6 sessions, I carved out opportunities for them to engage with one another's work, and consider: Did they like something specific about a classmate's puppet? Would they like to offer constructive suggestions to make someone else's puppet look or work better?

Such conversations helped children develop a capacity to learn from and support each other. For example, one student was appreciative of how another had combined a land animal (deer) and sea creature (fish). But she did not stop there.

She went on to recommend that perhaps her classmate might consider adding deer limbs to the fish body:

"So [your] animal will move in [both] water and land, and [this will] make it more powerful".

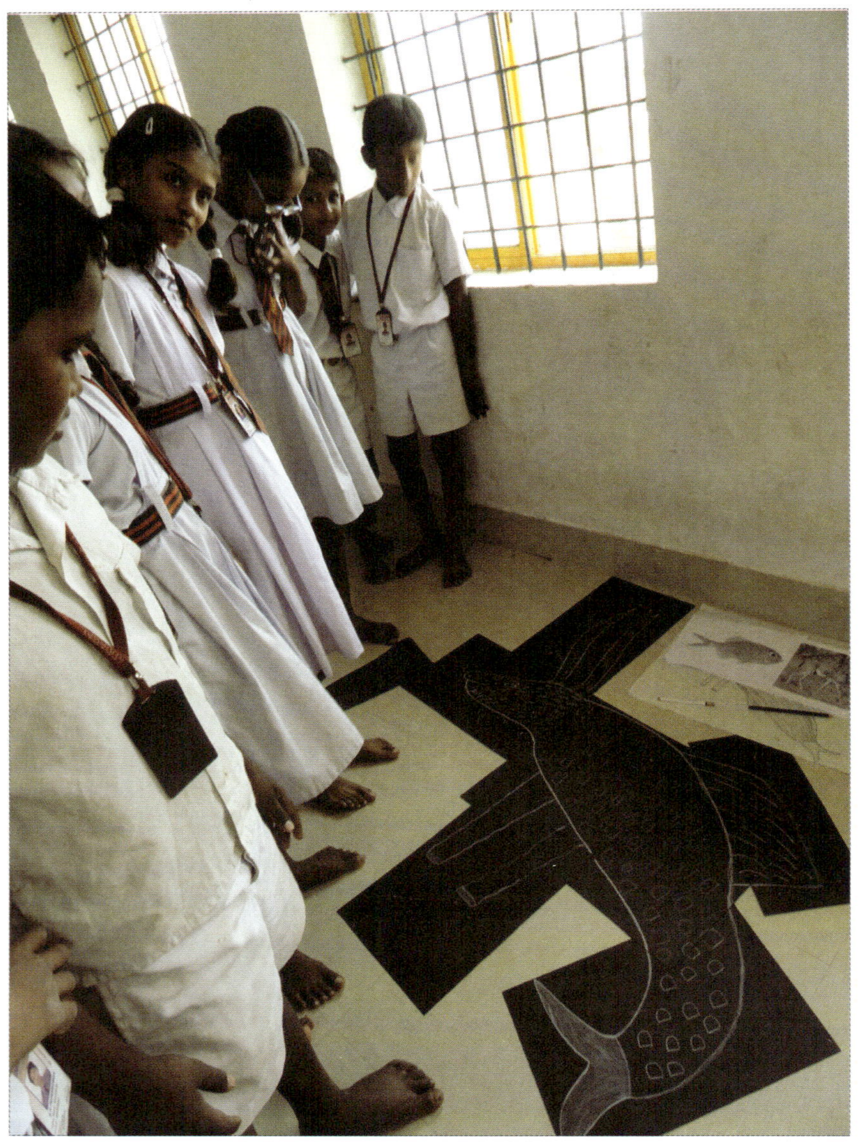

Working on an art project over a period of time provided students with plenty of opportunities to reflect on what they were doing, revisiting what they had done. It also provided them opportunities to assess what creative strategies worked for them and what did not. You could encourage this reflective process by posing questions such as these: "Is there anything else you would like to add? What? Why? Is there anything you would like to change? What will you do next?" Self-reflection when combined with peer assessment enable students to refine and even modify their work—a process that has value and relevance beyond the art classroom. Most important, it helps them to see mistakes as opportunities, and not barriers.

About Art

Exploring the interconnections between different forms of art can be
a very valuable exercise. For example, if children understand that shadow
puppet-making has its roots in drawing, they are bound to see and experience
drawing differently. Further, drawing ceases to be only a matter of skillful
rendering, of something, someone, or someplace. Instead it acquires a
purpose, that is, it ceases to be an end in itself, and becomes an activity
that can lead to other equally creative outcomes.

About the Learning Process

Art-making is a complex multidimensional process. Children need
help in staying engaged with it and also to persevere through complex
tasks. Thoughtfully structured art experiences can offer children a rich
space for such learning. In the art classroom with the 6th standard students,
it meant engaging the children in a multi-step process that required them
to stay on course, over a period of time, from start to finish. Since I had
arranged the learning tasks in such a manner that they increased gradually
in complexity - from initial rough sketches to final shadow puppets -
the children stayed challenged, but were not therefore overwhelmed
by the task at hand.

Building a sequential lesson plan is important for other reasons as well.
It allows the teacher to include opportunities for the children to go back
and revisit concepts, so that if necessary they could rethink their individual
solutions. Furthermore, this enables them to make decisions on their own,
become more self-reliant, rather than rely on the teachers' solutions.

As important as a structured learning activity, are unplanned for learning
moments—this happens when children aid each other. So make sure
that you provide opportunities for children to share their work with each
other. This opens them to additional possibilities, while fostering a culture
of shared learning and support.

Exploring Patterns

Once the puppets were completed, I introduced yet another task. I reminded the children of something they had noticed during the observational drawing phase: the ways in which animal skins were intricately patterned. To develop their puppets further, I suggested, they might want to learn about patterns and how to create them.

Let's look at his uniform. Does it have any designs?

3 of the 32 children in class raised their hands:

"Checks."

What shape are these checks?

"Square."

If I were to say his uniform has an interesting pattern, what is pattern?

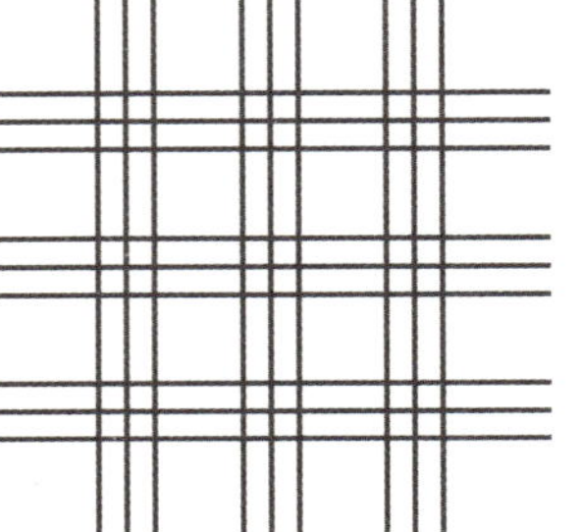

"Checks in uniform is pattern."

"Pattern is design."

To ensure that all the children clearly understood what patterns were, I shared two close-up images of animal hides:

What pattern does the zebra have on its body?

"Zebra pattern is stripes!"

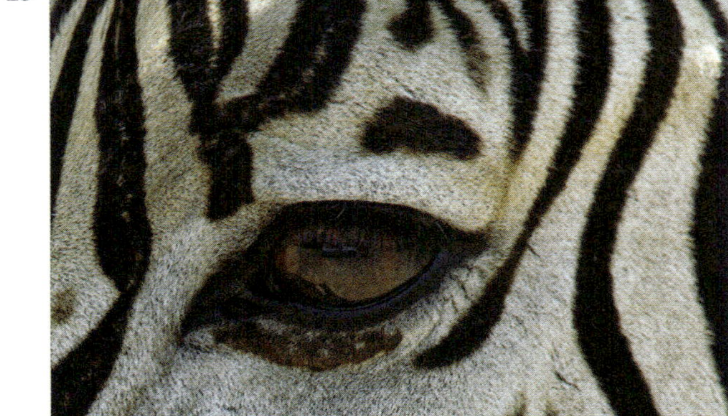

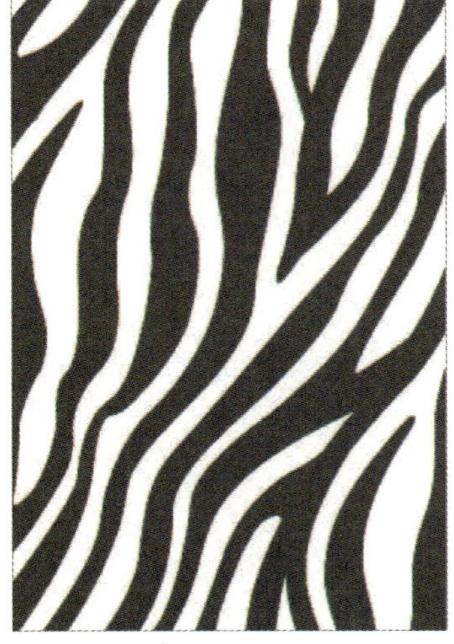

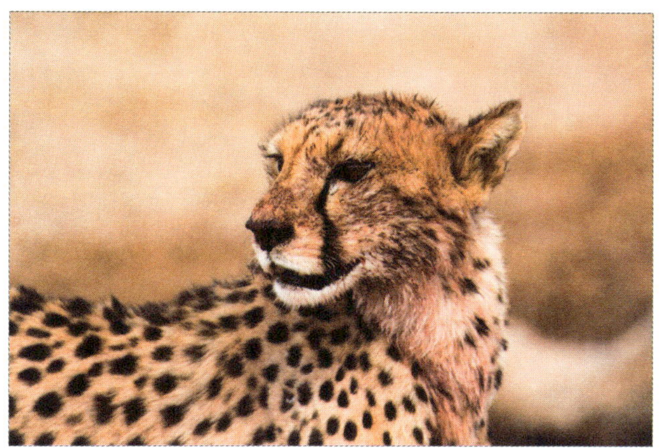

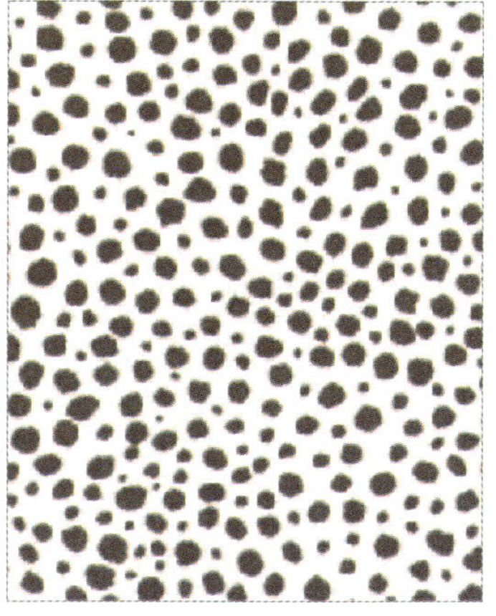

What about the cheetah?

So now we will see how to add patterns to make your puppets. Patterns will make your puppets visually interesting,
I added.

The next step was to come up with appropriate patterns and as we had done earlier, we brainstormed collectively for a while before the children sat down to decorate their puppets.

To enable the children to recognise more subtle textural patterns on an animal's skin, I brought out an image of a rhinoceros.

If we touch a rhinoceros, what would its skin feel like? Rough or smooth? Touch your own skin and then look at the picture again—is the rhino's skin rougher than yours or softer?

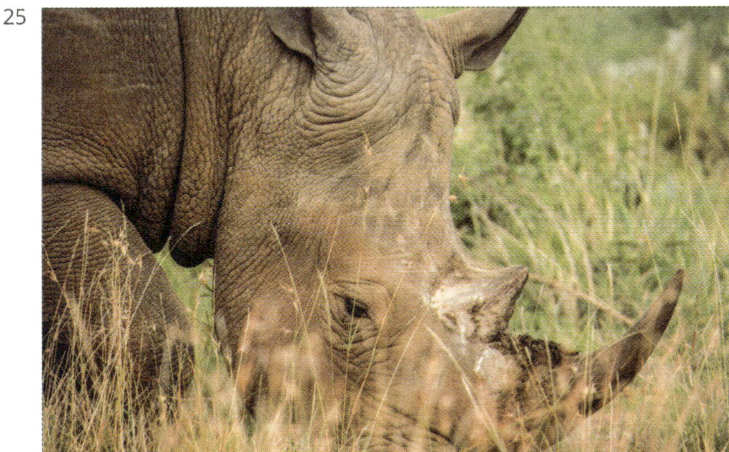

The children did as they were told. They felt their arms and faces, and then leaned in to look closely at the reference image.

"Rough!"
they responded in unison.

What makes you say that?

I wanted to make sure that the children remembered what they had learnt earlier: that every claim had to be backed by evidence.

"It looks rough."

"Rhinoceros skin has many lines."

"The [rhinoceros] skin has lot of bumps."

I then re-introduced the idea of "texture" to them: as a word that helps us comprehend the feel of skin or a surface. To further their understanding of texture, I showed the children two additional images, one of a camel and the other a frog.

26 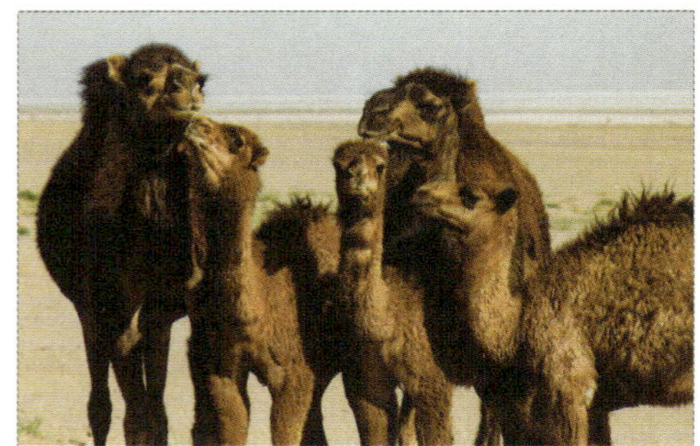 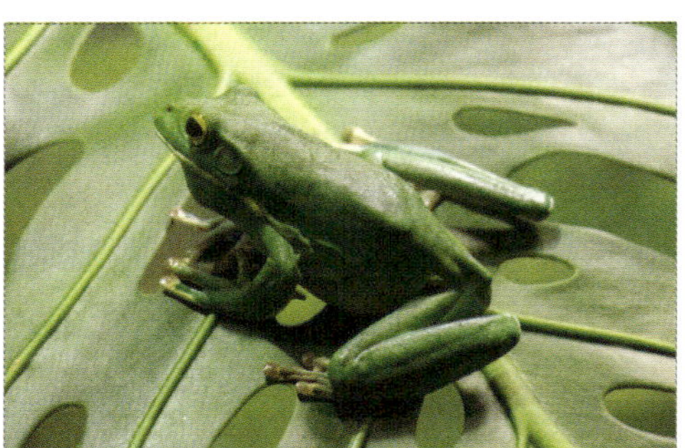 27

Does a camel and a frog feel the same? Do they have the same texture?

The children unanimously responded,
"No!"

Pressing further, I asked:
Why do they feel different?

"Frog has wet skin. It is slippery."

"A camel has hair. Hair is rough."

My next task was to link these conversations on texture to the idea of a pattern—to demonstrate how textures could be represented as simple and stylised patterns.

I picked up my own hybrid camel puppet and asked the children:
How do I show that the camel has rough skin?

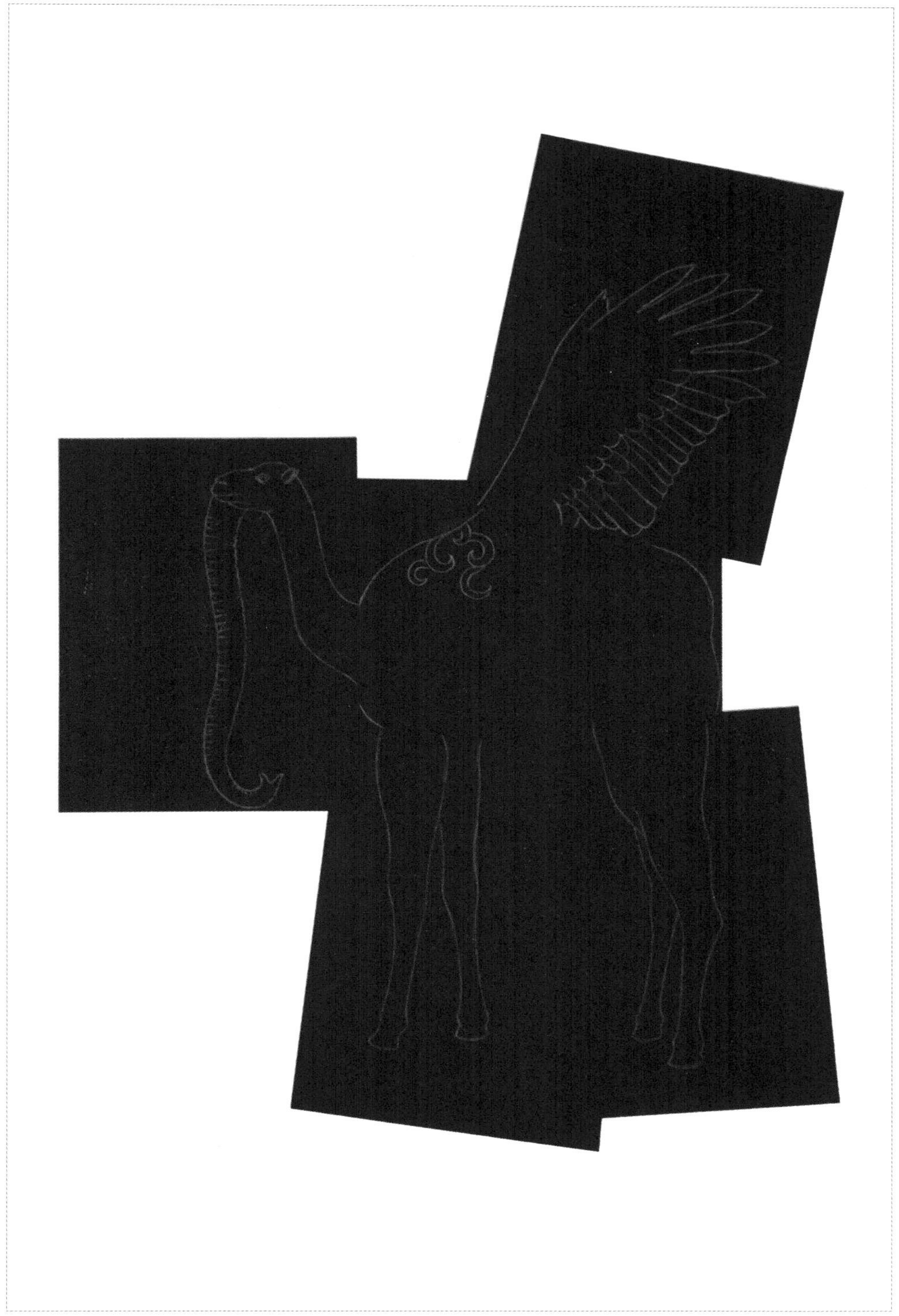

To make sure that the children knew what I was talking about, I put my puppet aside and showed them the close-up photograph of the camel.

What lines and shapes should I use to draw the camel's skin texture?

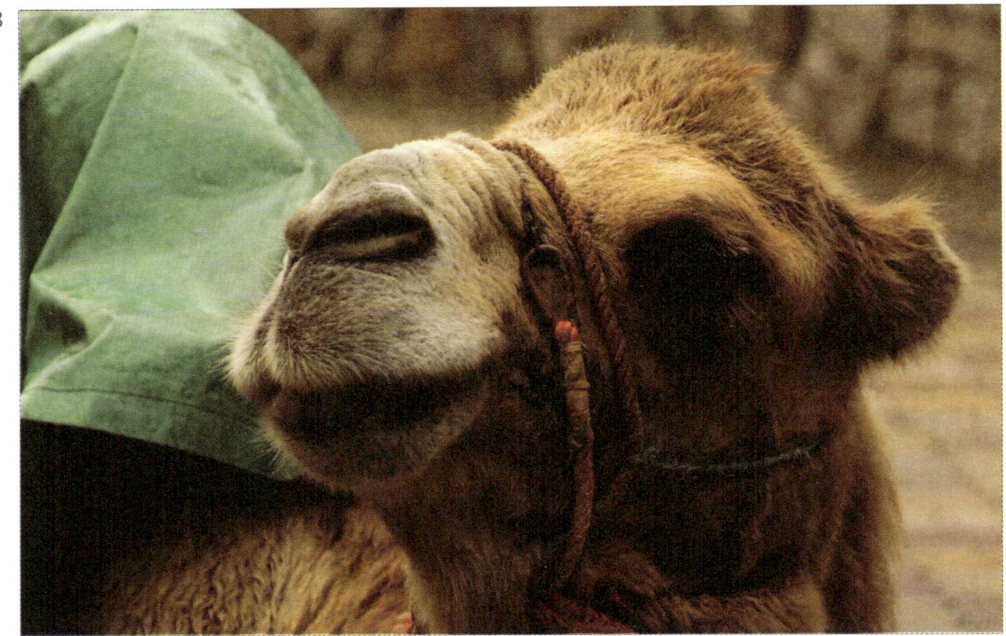

28

The children immediately responded.

"I see curly lines."

"[Camel] hair has wavy lines."

"[The] hair is a ring shape."

Gesturing with his finger, one child drew a free-form shape in the air and said,

"Hair is [a] shape like this."

As the children offered suggestions I began to add lines and draw shapes onto my sample puppet to construct its surface pattern. As before, I modelled active decision-making, so that the children noticed how the varied patterns I drew interacted with one another; and also how I covered some parts of the puppet while leaving others untouched.

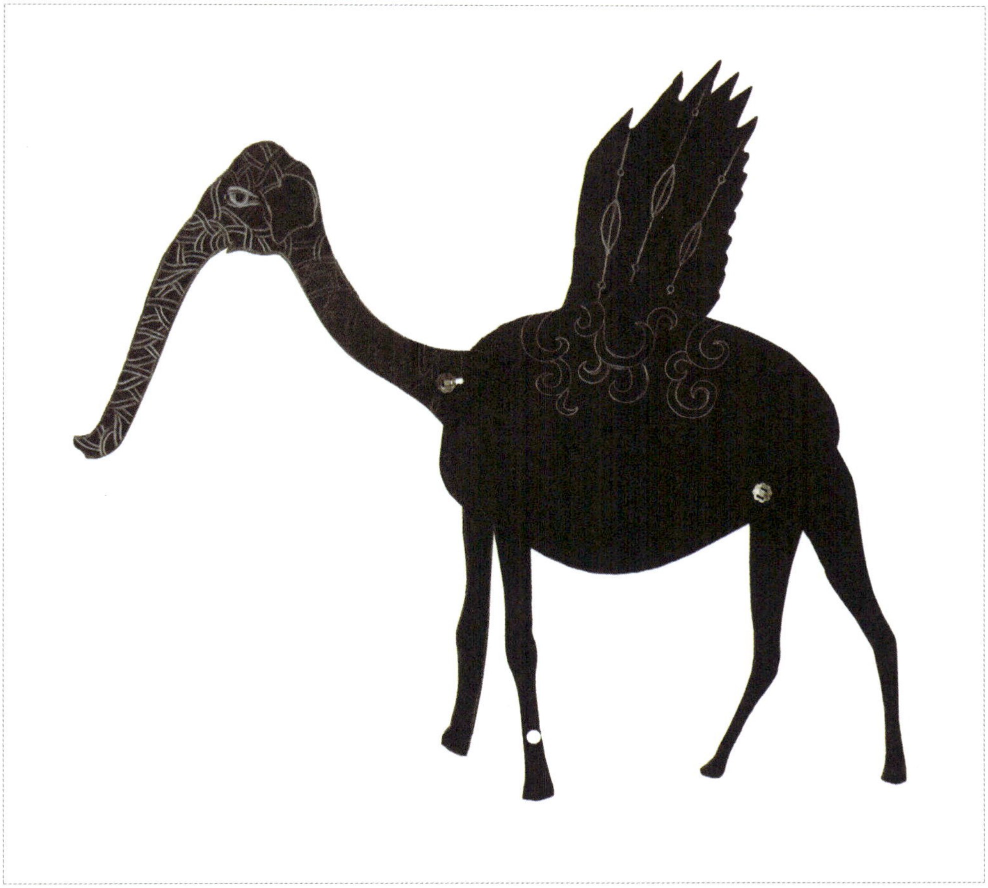

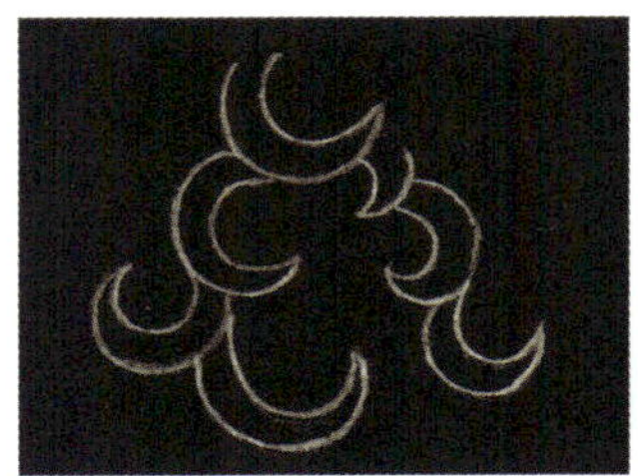 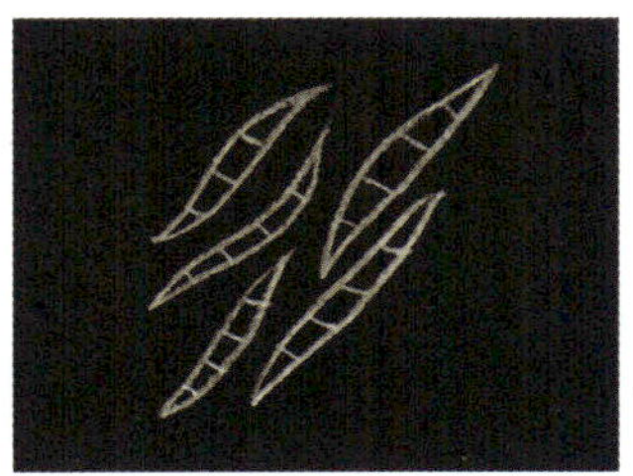 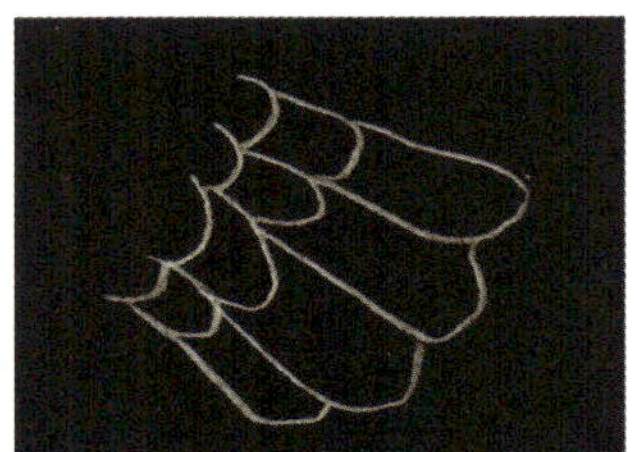

When you demonstrate creating patterns, make sure that children notice where you place them—especially why they ought to be enclosed within the puppet form. It is important for them to also understand why you have done this. It might be a good idea to share a picture of a shadow puppet with surface patterns, and ask questions that enable children to recognise how some parts have been cut out for light to shimmer through. Also when you cut out patterns in your sample puppet, make sure you involve the children in deciding what patterns to cut. This will help them understand what works and what does not.

When the children sat down to work on their own puppets, it was evident that they had a clear understanding of what patterns were.

In fact, no child's pattern was like another's. Some modelled their patterns on the animal's skin texture. Others abstracted from what they observed and gave free vent to their imagination. For example, two children had created hybrid lion puppets, but the surface patterns they drew were very different. One child chose to depict her lion's mane using long sinuous lines to create enclosed shapes that had the appearance of thick flowing strands of hair. Another chose to abstract her lion's mane, using slim rectangular shapes to depict the strands of hair.

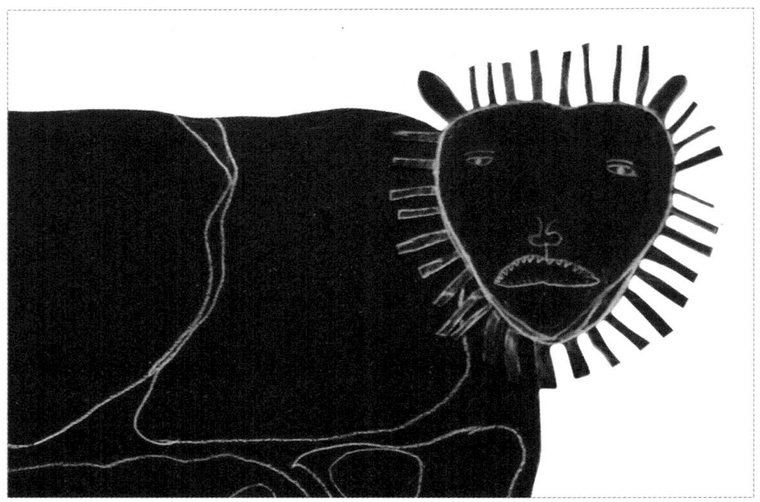

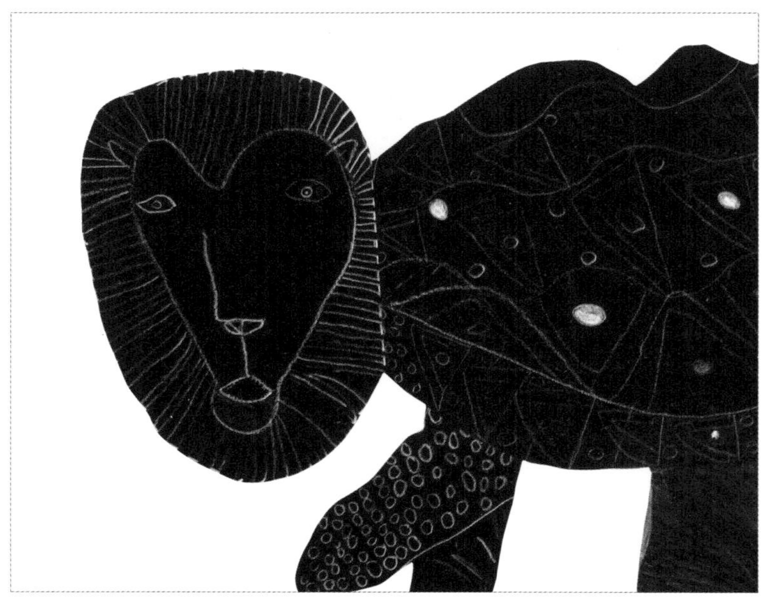

The children had clearly made thoughtful decisions about what lines
and shapes to combine. As one child noted, while describing her puppet:

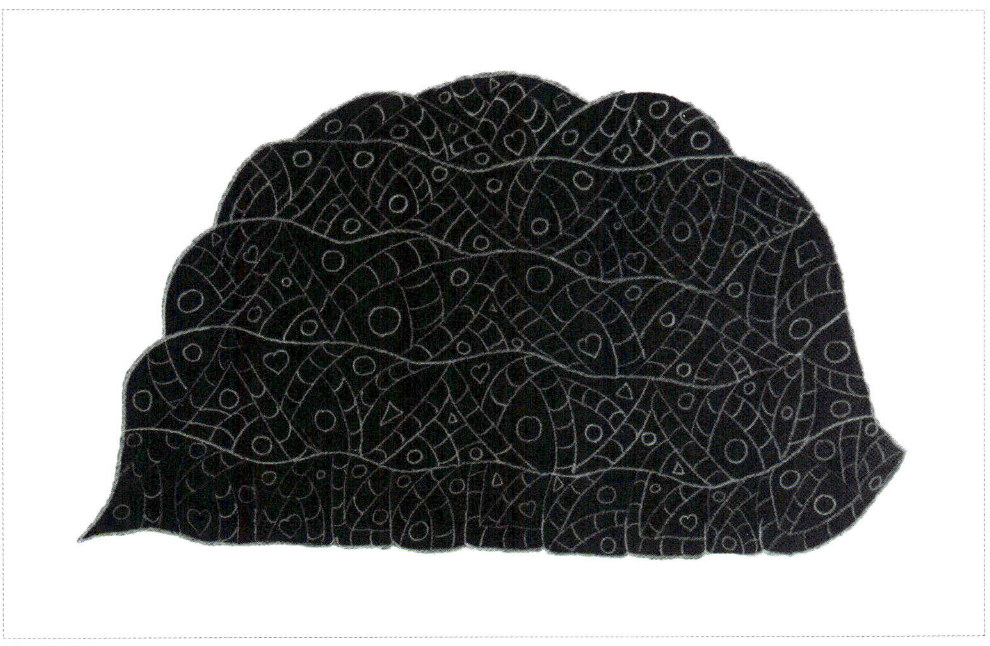

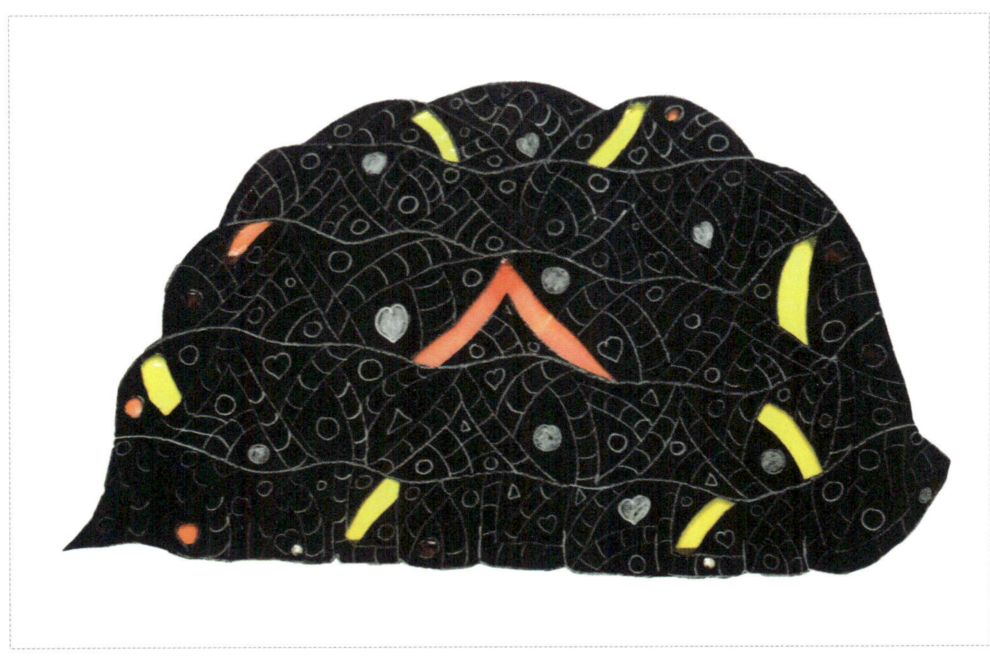

About Art

As artists hone their abilities to look closely and observe details,
they begin to recognise patterns in everything. Investigation plays an
important role in enabling an artist to combine lines and shapes in varied
ways to re-create observed patterns. Some artists go beyond what they
have observed and seek to invent patterns by freely exploring and
experimenting with lines, shapes, and their various configurations.

About the Learning Process

Providing children with opportunities to explore pattern-making develops
their capacities to look closely and carefully and to translate what they
see into stylised lines and shapes. It also gives them a chance to experiment
and to invent as they go along. Importantly, children who engage in these
processes learn to entertain multiple possibilities, work at diverse solutions,
and shift course in the middle of what they are doing to adopt entirely
new approaches to their work.

To nurture and foster these artistic behaviours in the art classroom,
this is what I kept in mind. You might want to adapt these strictures to
your own purpose:

- Reassure children that in the realm of investigation, there are no right
  or wrong answers. There are just endless possibilities. Therefore, it is
  perfectly acceptable to try something out and then change course.

- Let children know that investigations must result in a minimum
  stipulated number of discoveries. And, that their discoveries need to
  be distinct. This pushes children to remain open to possibilities and
  yet set themselves a goal.

- You might also want to respond to children's work processes in ways
  that help them build on what they have achieved. That is, you could help
  them become more intentional with their work. For example, you could
  say: "I notice that you are using your white pencil lightly to create thin,
  light, wavy lines to show the hair on your lions head. I also notice that

you are pressing down on your white pencil to get darker
and thicker lines to show the rough texture on your tortoises' legs."
Such comments encourage children to actively think about the
choices that they're making.

- Make sure that you avoid giving children concrete suggestions to
  follow. Instead put forth questions that encourage children to think for
  themselves, and come up with their own solutions. For example, you
  could say: "I notice you used a lot of wavy lines as well as small circles to
  show the rough and bumpy texture of the tortoise' shell. What types of
  lines and shapes will you use to show the Zebra's head and neck?"

- Provide opportunities for children to share their discoveries
  with others. This opens them to additional possibilities, while fostering
  a culture of shared learning and support.

EXPLORING LANGUAGE DEVELOPMENT

Communicate

How can art offer rich opportunities to develop children's language and communication skills?

Communication is an essential component of an artist's practice, and artists often communicate through different means. For example, they may communicate non-verbally through their artworks, so much so, that when we view a piece of art, the artwork often "speaks" to us. Occasionally, visual cues present in an artwork may help in the communication process. Artists also communicate verbally by engaging in dialogue with others. Through this process of dialogue, artists articulate their intent, receive and respond to feedback, and practice active listening. Furthermore, artists communicate with the help of the written word, using artist statements, for example, to shed more light upon their work.

Developing communication skills in children is, and should be, an important goal of education. The capacity to communicate effectively enables us to connect and engage more deeply with others. Usually the language classroom is associated with communication. Equally, the art classroom is a valuable and authentic space to develop this skill.

The challenge for the art teacher is to ensure that children learn to articulate their thoughts, ideas and opinions clearly to others, and, develop an ability to listen. Children's personal involvement with their artworks can help in this process as they talk about what they have done, solicit ideas from others, and share their opinions. In such instances, their use of language tends to be more imaginative as well.

Considering Characters and Stories

With the 6th standard students that I worked with, puppet-making provided an ideal context for us to explore different aspects of communication. In fact, I introduced puppet-making as an activity with the intent of developing the children's expressive capacities. I wanted them to speak freely, and engage with language creatively. Since the children were English language learners, I encouraged them to speak in both English and their native language, or even mix the two up depending on their comfort level. I did not want them to feel constrained by notions of right and wrong usage.

As an introduction to characters and character traits, I began with a series of questions about animals in general:

Is a lion strong or weak?

What about a zebra?

Is a tortoise friendly or scary?

The children's responses included:

"No, a tortoise is very friendly."

"It is shy."

"It is not scary."

"[A] lion is scary. It is strong."

"It is eating other animals."

"Zebra is very kind."

"[Zebra is] very beautiful."

My next set of questions had to do with hybrid animals. I wanted the children to get comfortable defining and constructing the personality of an imaginary hybrid animal character. My intent was to also enable them to eventually assign distinct characteristic traits to their own puppet characters.

I wonder, what kind of personality a half lion, half tortoise would have?

A child responded,
"[A] half lion half tortoise will be kind and friendly with everybody. But it will scare someone if they attack. [The] hunter will not know that the lion is inside [the] tortoise shell. He will try and attack [the] tortoise. But he will be scared by [the] lion."

Another said,
"[This] animal will be kind. It will be eating only fruits. But many animals will be very scared because of lion. Lion is looking very strong."

A third noted:
"Tortoise is kind. It has [a] shell. It is walking slowly. Lion is strong. It is running fast. It will eat other animals."

Eliciting at least two to three different responses from the children helped reinforce that all responses received, from the literal to the more imaginative, were valid.

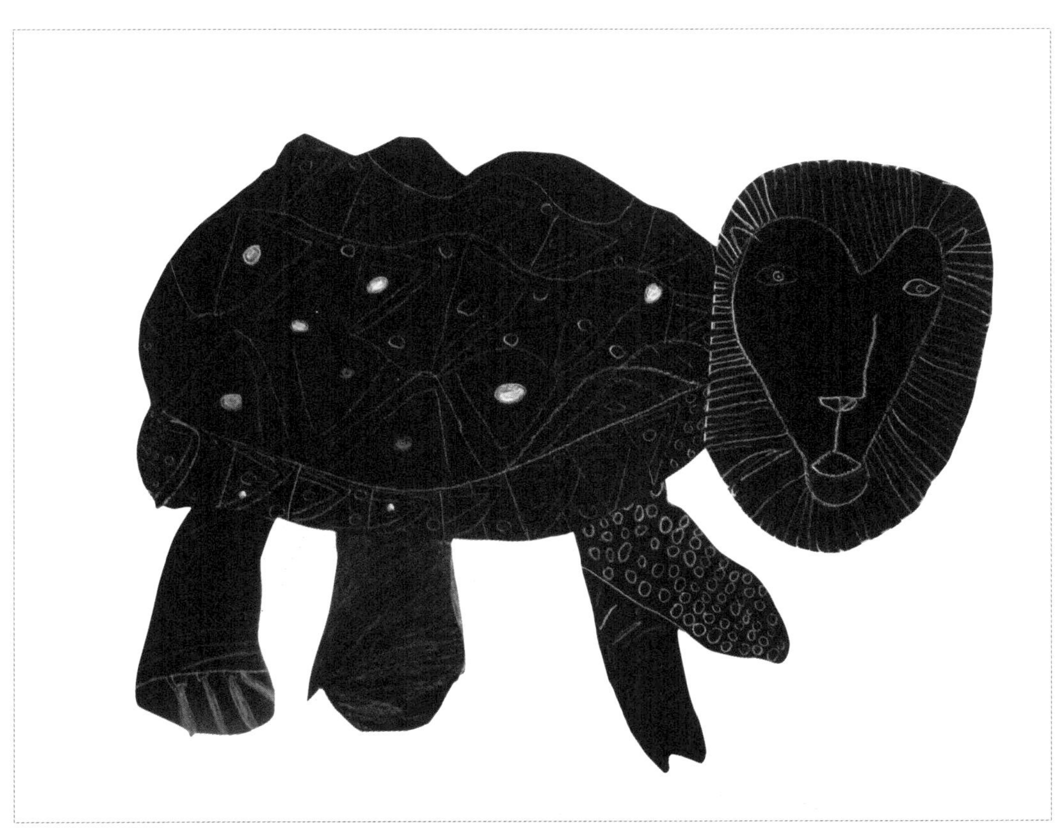

This discussion paved the way for the children to revisit their own hybrid animal puppets, and construct their own characters. Clearly the children's enthusiasm for their puppets made them less inhibited when speaking. I could sense a growing confidence in them, as they described their hybrid animals. They were not intimidated about using the English language and were happily imaginative.

For example, one child described her hybrid animal thus:
"Rooster will not fly up like many birds. But my rooster and frog animal will use frog legs and will jump very high, and also it will climb the wall. If danger is there, my animal will go fast and call to people to be safe."

Another had this to say about his animal:
"Goat and fish animal will live in water and will live in land. If lion or cheetah or other animal will attack, it will go in water and save itself."

Once the children had a sense of their characters and their traits, I decided that it was time for them to develop a character outline. I asked the children to write down descriptions of their puppet characters.

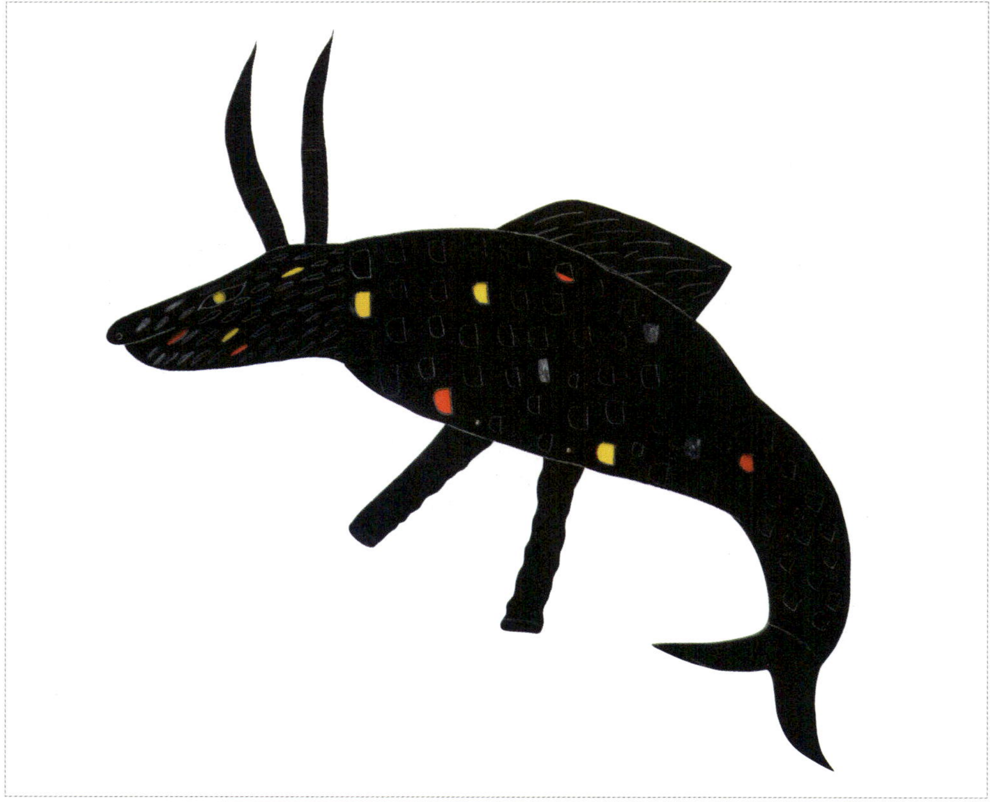

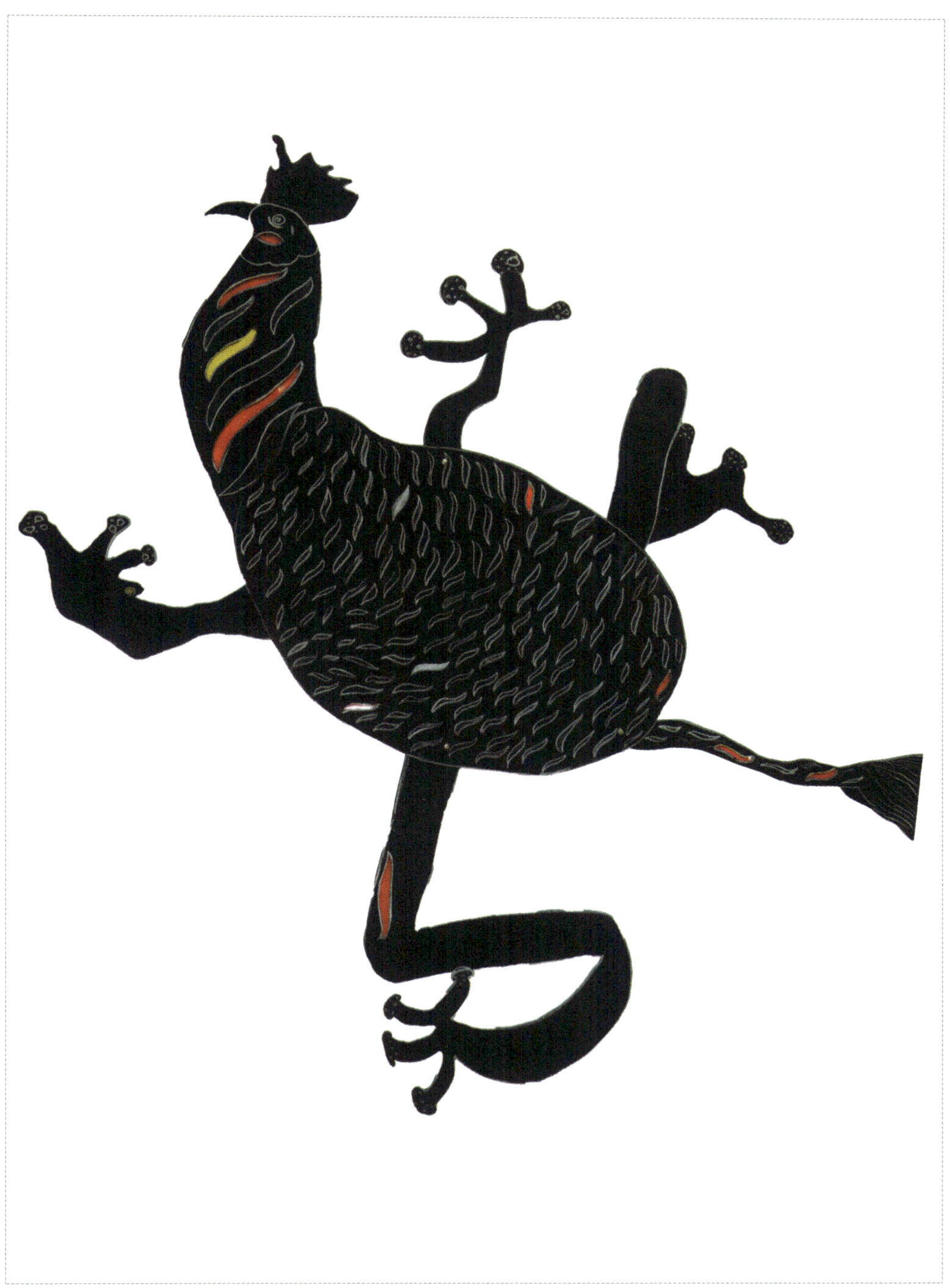

While encouraging children to write about their puppet characters, it is important to remember that the aim of the writing component is not to judge the children on the accuracy of their writing. It is to provide children with opportunities to put aside their inhibitions and build confidence gradually as they engage with language.

Once this was done, I went on to discuss key aspects of storytelling.
I started off, sharing a sequence of stills from an animation.

What do you think is happening here?

"Deer is living in [the] forest. He is very happy."

"Hunters will catch the deer in net."

"All the hunters and people are taking [the] deer to the palace."

"They will be giving [the] deer to [the] king."

"King is looking at [the] deer."

"Deer is in [the] cage, and they will kill the deer and eat the deer.
Deer is very sad."

The children were connecting what they were seeing, from one
frame to the next. I encouraged them to go further and expand on their
observations, paying particular attention to the different characters in
the story. The children went on to say:

"Hunters [are] like Rakshasas (demons)."

"The hunters are scaring all animals.
They are catching deer and taking to the king."

"King is very rich."

I shifted to other aspects of the story.

Who is the main character? How can you tell?

"Deer is [the] main [character]. It is in all pictures,"

"King is very powerful. He is very rich. He is main person."

Drawing on the children's responses, I pointed to different elements
that make up a story: characters, setting, and plot. I then went on to
share a second series of stills, to demonstrate how different stories
unfold differently.

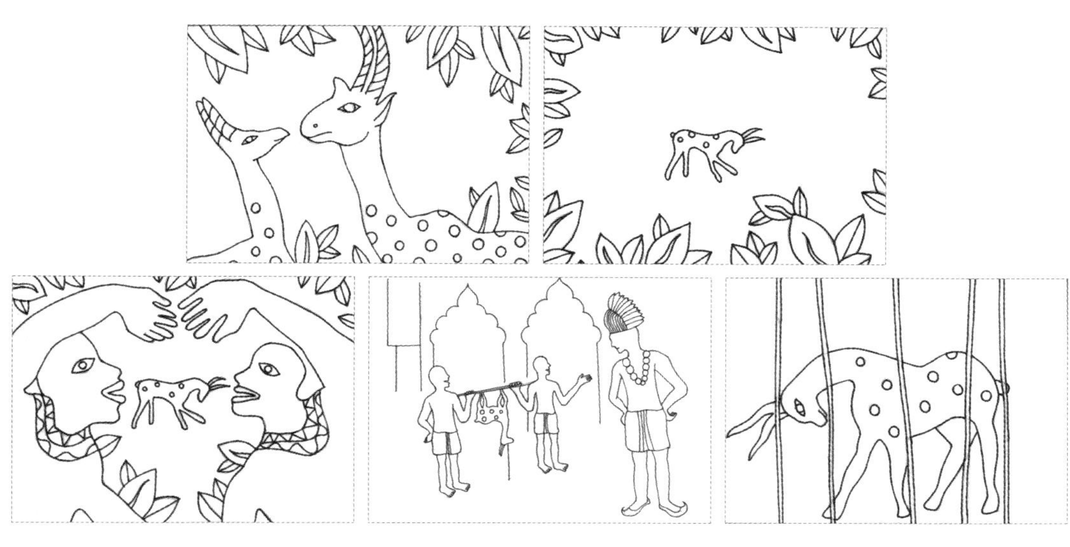

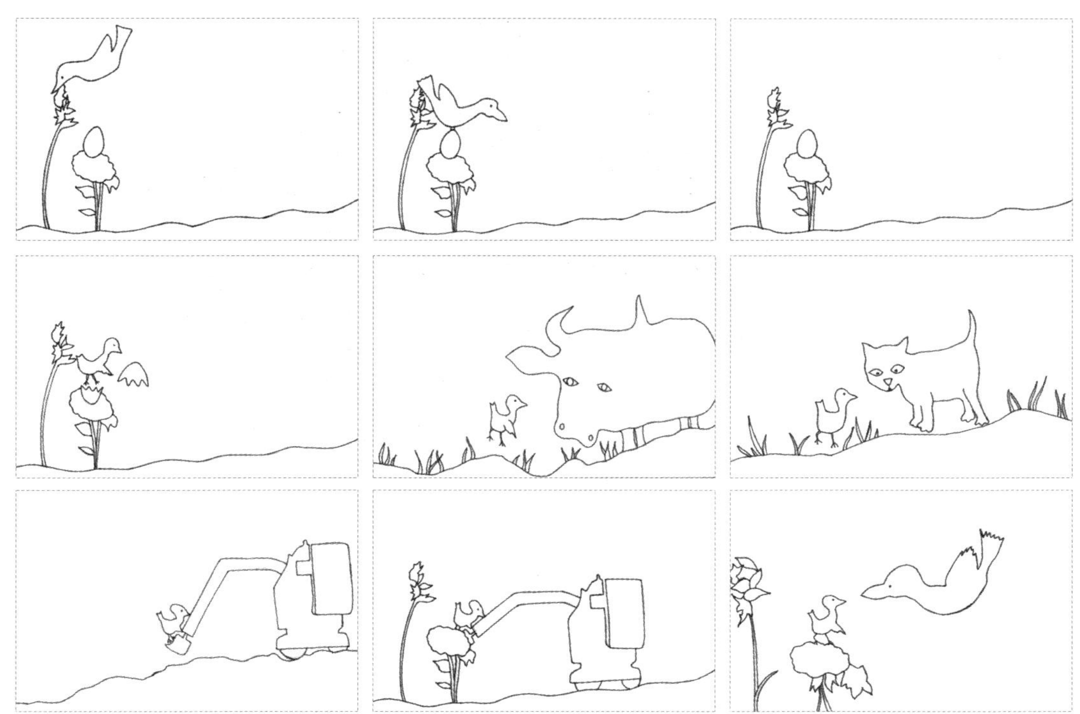

The children then got together in small groups to construct simple stories involving their puppet characters. The idea was to get children within each group to speak of their individual puppet characters and come up with a story that featured all of them. This is how the storytelling process unfolded:

Students in a particular group introduced their hybrid animal puppets to one another. This helped everyone in the group to familiarise themselves with the characters that they would be working with. The group members then proceeded to brainstorm, making sure that all the children in the group had a chance to speak and share their story ideas.

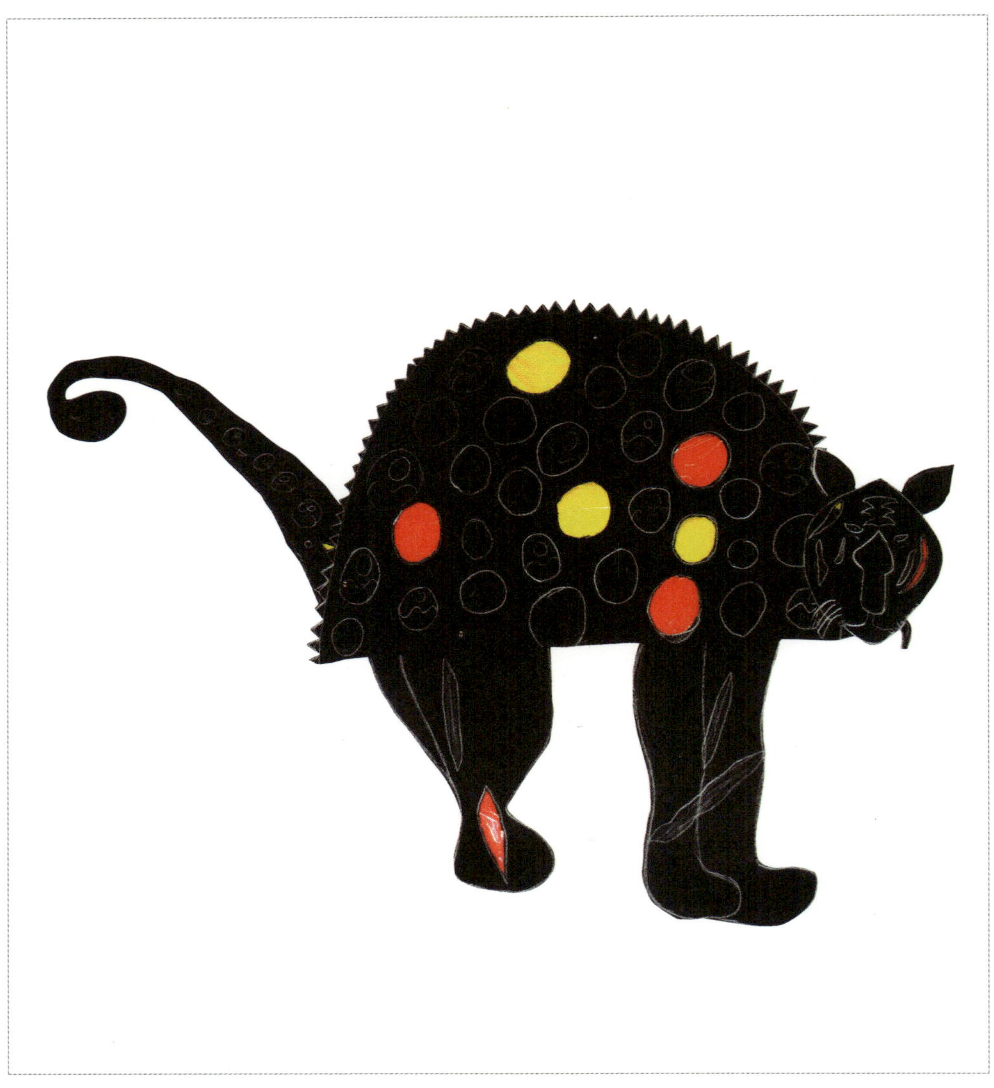

Once several story options were presented, the children voted on the story they would focus on. After this, they discussed the sequence of events that make up a story. Following this, everyone in the group had a chance to refine the story: add in details of the setting; details of particular scenes; tweak characters, and so on. After the story was finished to everyone's satisfaction, one student within each group, took on the responsibility of writing it down.

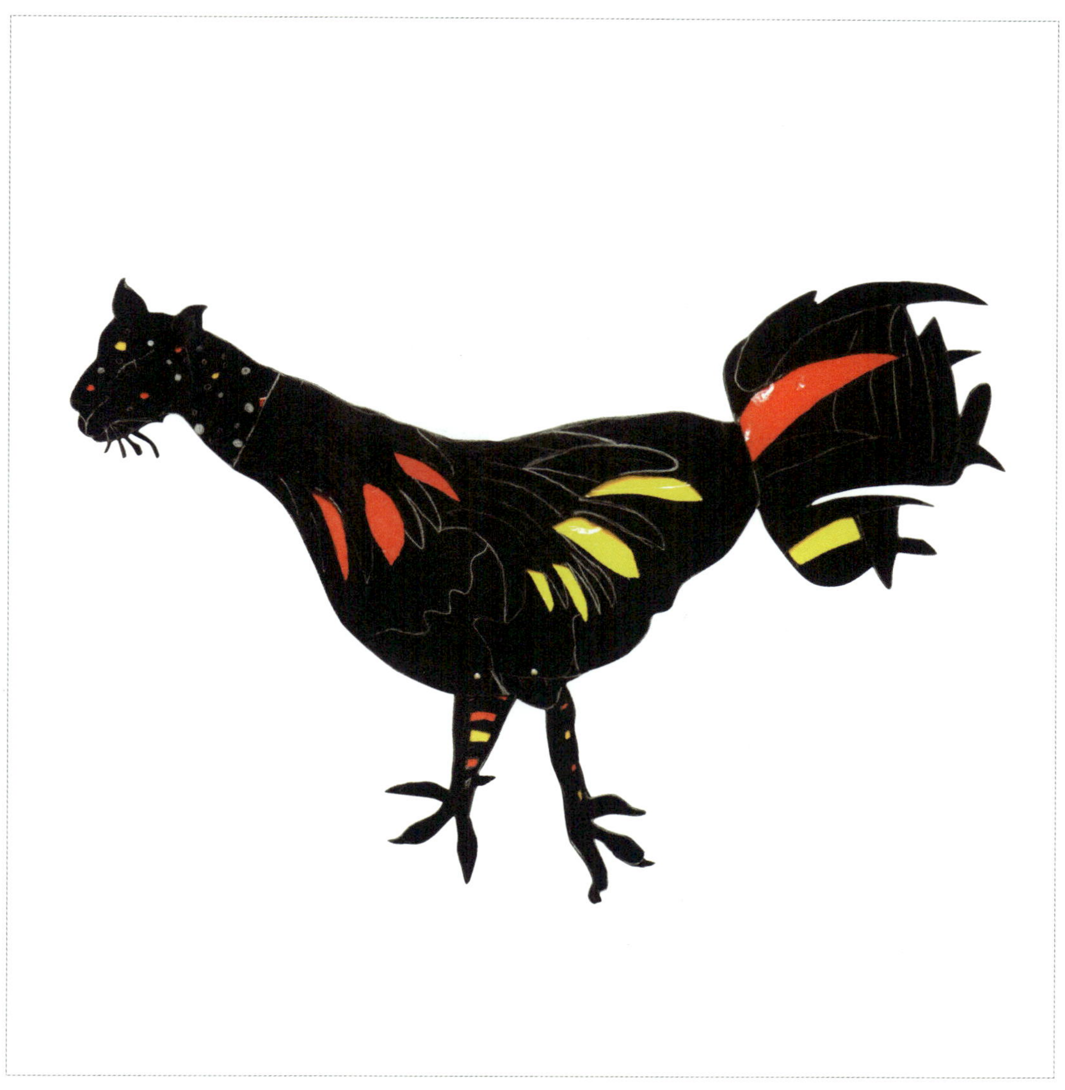

Children's Stories

STORY I

Once upon a time there was a big forest. In that forest many animals were living. Four of the animals were very different from the others. They were hybrid animals. One of them was named Manju, it had a buffalo's face and an elephant's body.

One day an animal named Shashi, which had a tiger's face and hippopotamus' body, went to drink water near the lake.

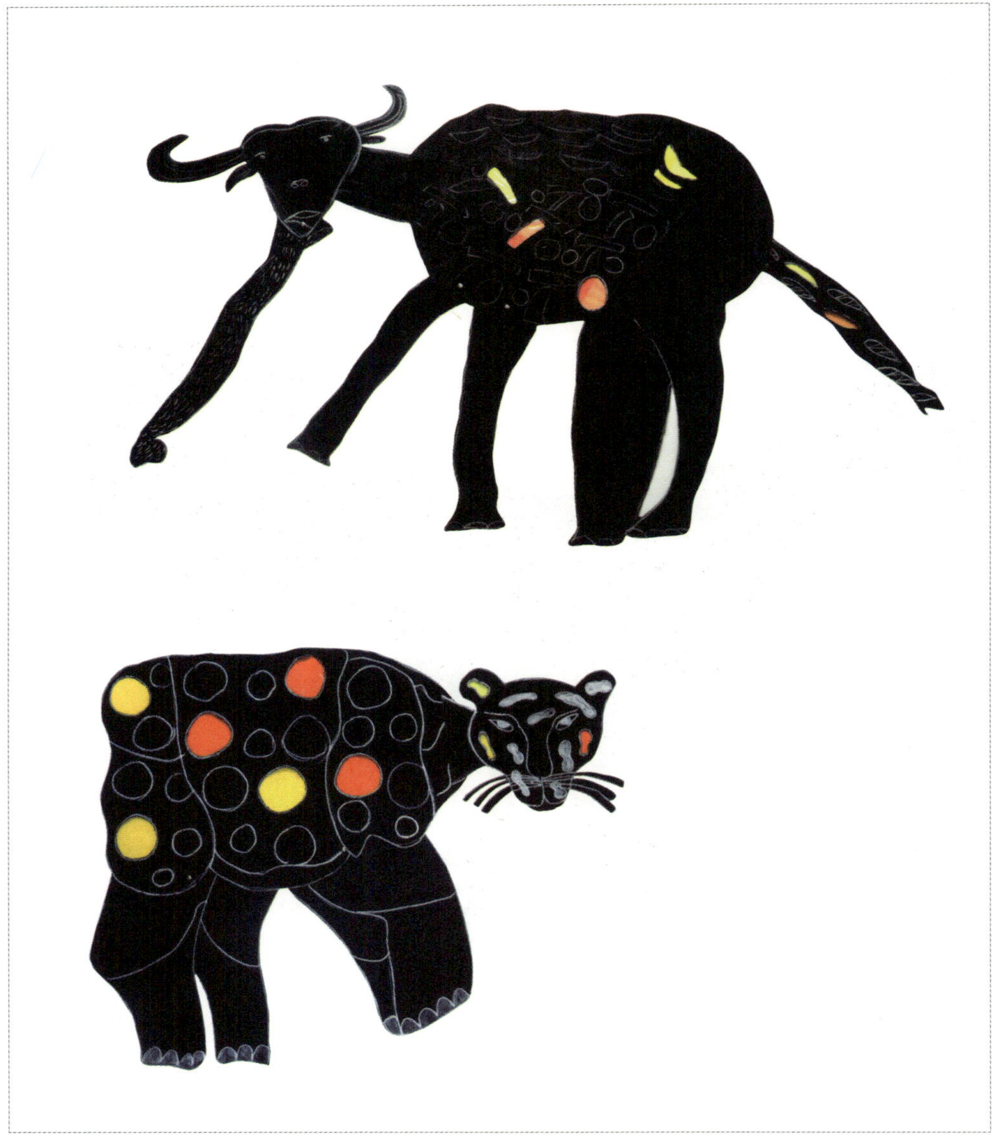

He slipped and fell into that lake. Manju saw this and got afraid, then quickly called his two friends Chandu and Chukki. Chandu had a lions face and elephant's body. Chukki had a cheetah's face and fish's body. Chukki was able to swim. Chandu was strong. With their help, Shashi came out of the lake.

Manju brought some medicine and kept it ready. Manju treated Shashi with the medicine. After sometime Shashi became better. And the four friends feeling happy went off to play.

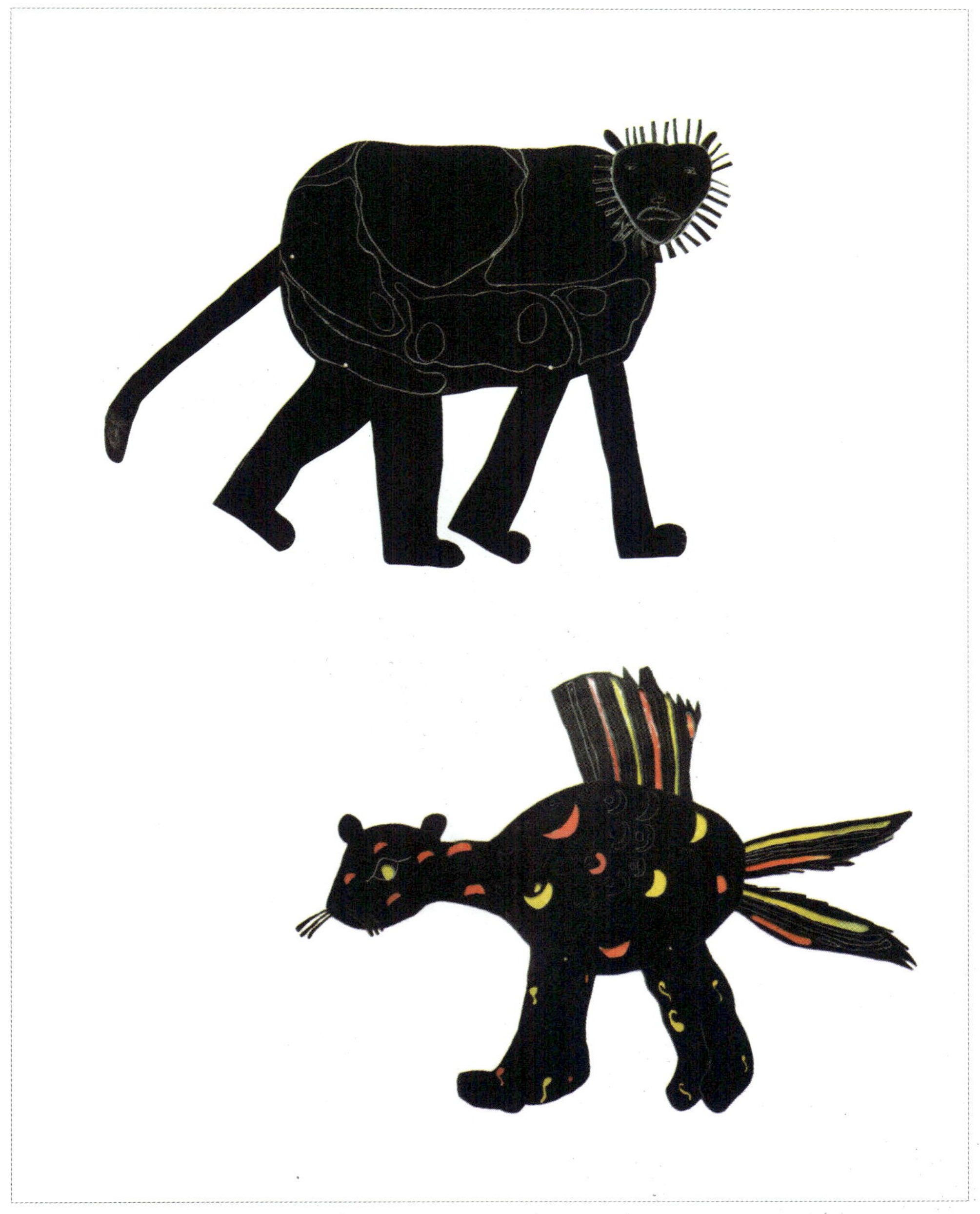

STORY 2

My hybrid animal character has a tortoise's body, zebra's head, leopard's tail and rooster's legs. The tortoise's body is smooth and hard and it has many patterns. It protects my character. The leopard's tail helps me if I want to scare someone. My character runs fast and it can eat all types of food. Totally my character is good and kind. My animal character can live on land and also in water.

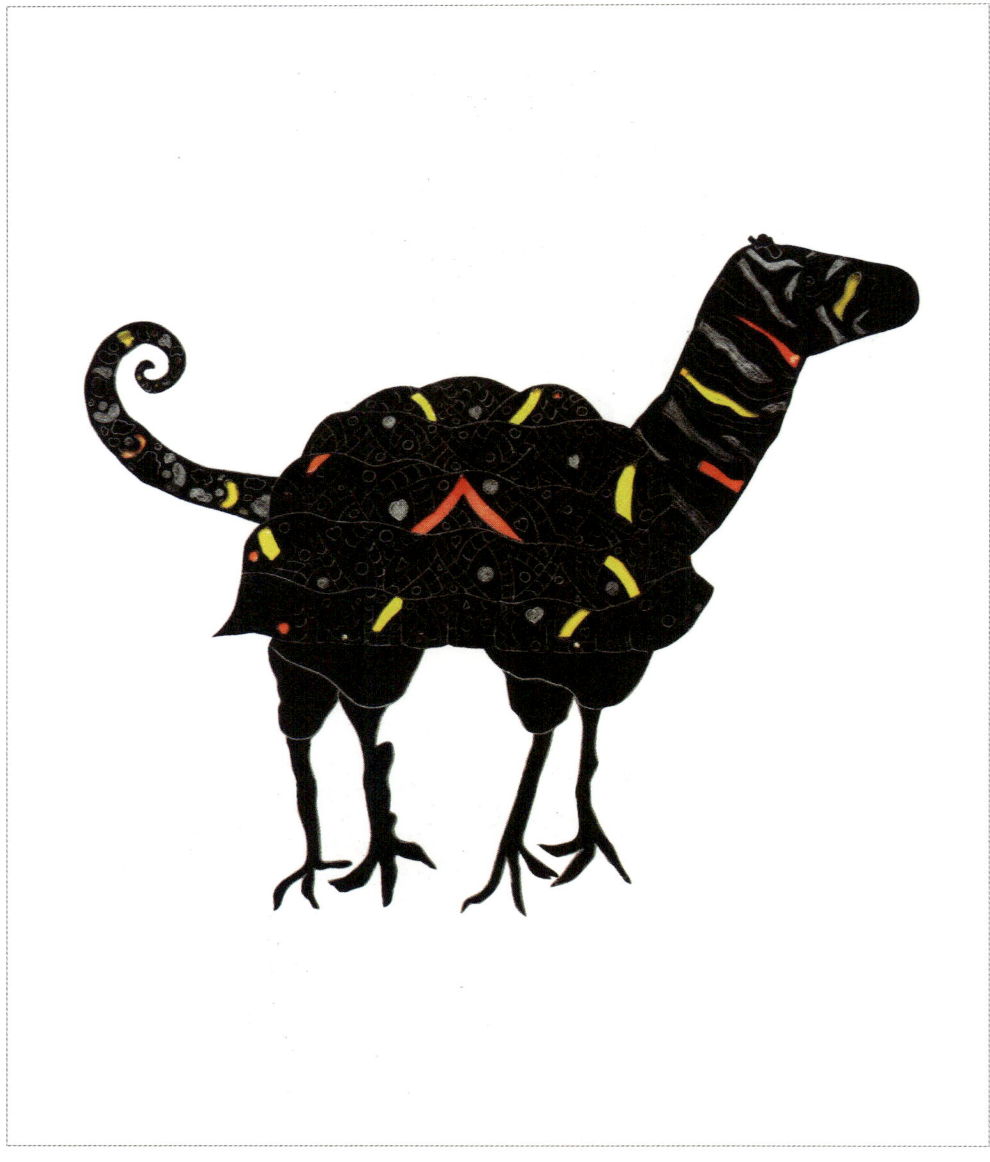

STORY 3

My imaginary animal has a frog's body, buffalo's head, and cheetah's tail.
The frog has a slippery body. The frog's colour is green. The frog is beautiful.
The frog's legs helps my animal jump far. The buffalo has strong horns.
It lives in the village. The buffalo is very fat and strong. It is black in colour.
It eats grass. The buffalo is a domestic animal. The buffalo's horns help
protect my imaginary animal. The cheetah is a wild animal. Its colour
is yellow. It also helps protect my animal.

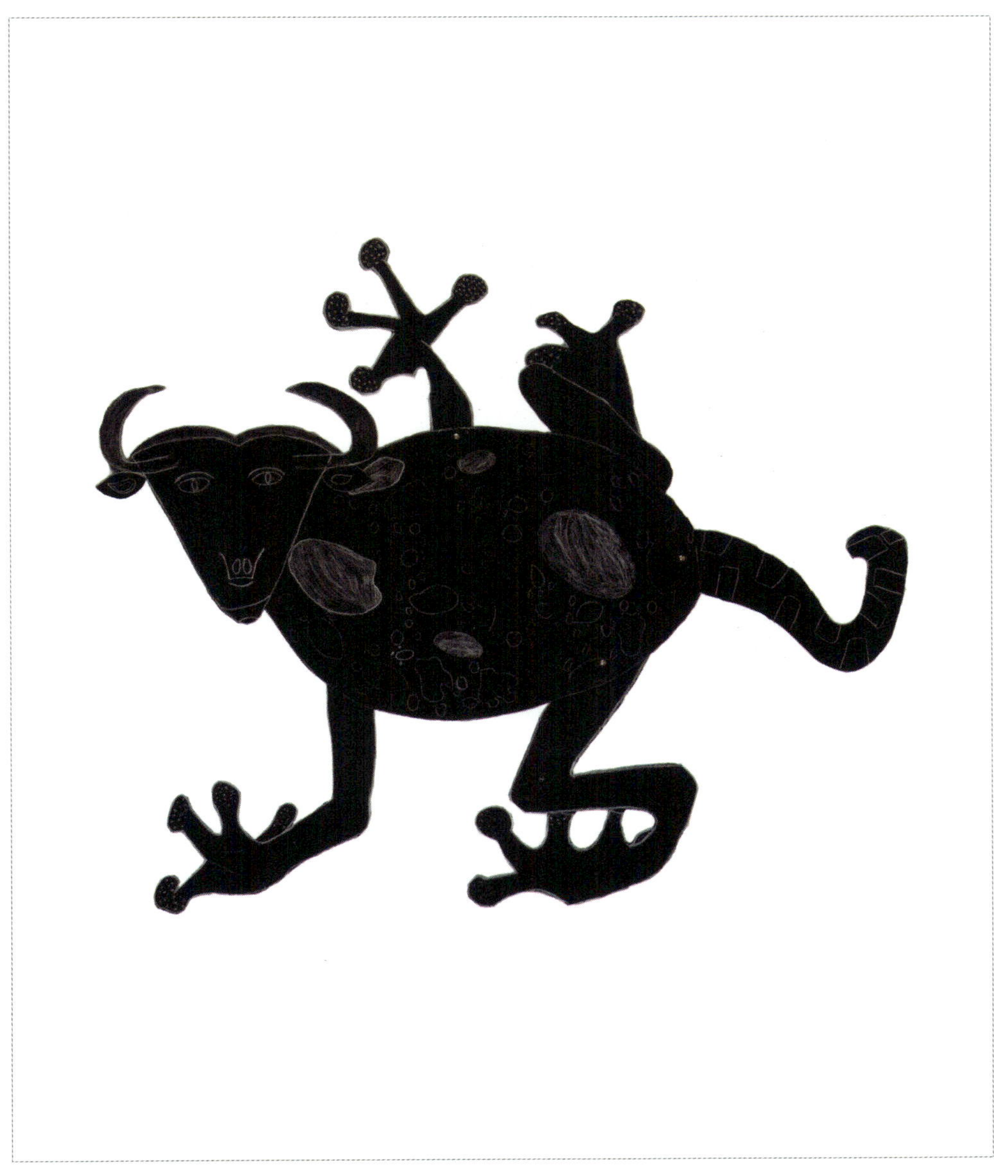

STORY 4

I combined a zebra and eagle to make my imaginary animal.
With the eagle wings, my imaginary animal can fly in the sky and
search for food. It can also help another animal and carry it
on its back and go from place to place.

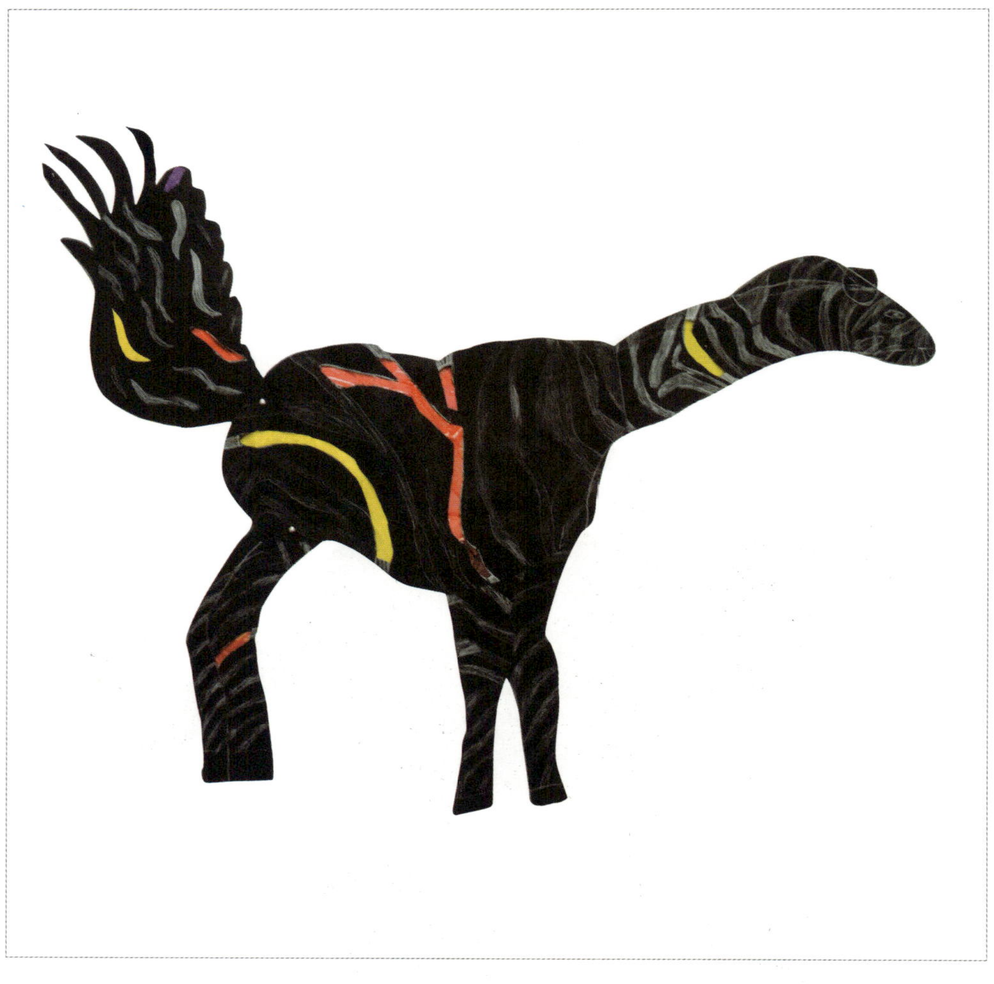

STORY 5

My imaginary animal is very kind. The elephant stores water in his trunk and gives it to others. The buffalo gives his milk to people to drink. With a chameleon's tail, my imaginary animal has the power to go from one place to another and change his body colour so the hunter does not see him.

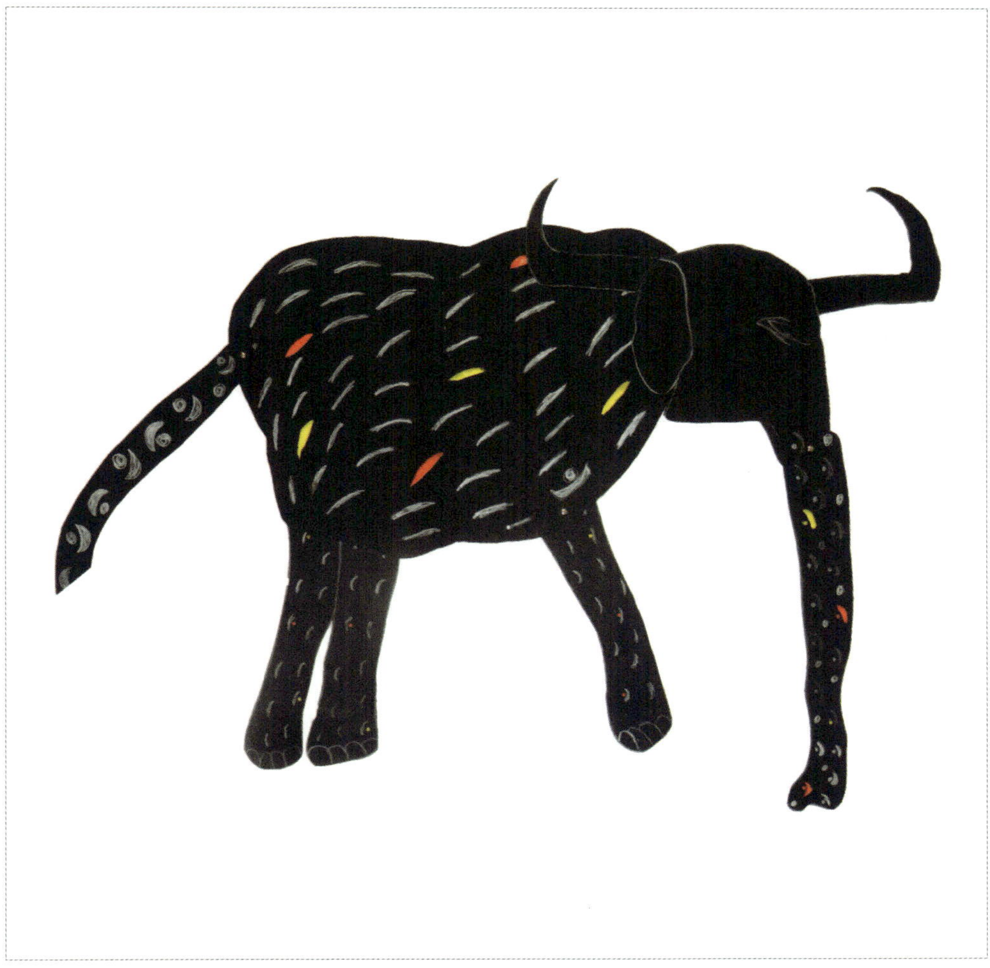

As children sit down to develop their puppet stories within their assigned groups, and get ready to practice performing, make sure that all their various skills are put to use. Give children (and their groups) the choice to develop their stories and perform in English, or perform in their native language, integrating English words and sentences based on their comfort level. The aim is to gently ease and encourage children to use English, not to intimidate them.

About Art

In India there exist distinct puppet forms, primarily used to tell stories: stories that recall history, stories that entertain, but also stories that inform. Puppets are thus highly effective visual aids that help support the communicative aspects of language. Also, they add a visually compelling and expressive dimension to storytelling.

Puppets are particularly useful in classrooms where children are too shy to speak or learning a new language that is not their own. As I learned from working with my 6th standard students, the puppets they made offered them just the right amount of support: children could speak of them, around them, and in many cases, use them to fill in the gaps that could not be bridged by language. Thus, they came to understand the symbiotic relationship between puppetry, language, and storytelling. For example, they learned how language could support art-making by communicating the intent of the artist. They also found out how an artwork could enable them to express their story ideas and emotions—thus, facilitating communication.

About the Learning Process

Encouraging children to create art and to develop narratives around their artwork advances language learning in a multitude of ways. For one, the sense of ownership that children feel in developing their own stories around an artwork they have created is very real. It enables children to more successfully shed inhibitions associated with using a language that is not their own. However, for this to happen, children need opportunities to develop their stories within a judgment-free environment that celebrates their efforts at storytelling.

Developing a story also requires children to delve into the elements of storytelling - character, plot, description - and put them to use in creating a story. Through this process, they get to internalise what they've learned, and slowly but surely, storytelling becomes a part of their repertoire of skills.

The Artist Exhibition

The work of an artist does not merely comprise of creating
an artwork. An artist often uses his or her work to communicate an idea,
a message, a feeling, with an audience. And artists exhibit their work
so that they can share it with others, have conversations around them,
and elicit varied responses.

In the case of children, an artists' exhibition serves a similar purpose:
it helps them communicate what they have created, and share their ideas.
It gives the audience an opportunity to celebrate the children's immense
efforts. But it can also do more: for example, it could be used to present
their artwork, as it evolved, from initial concept to completion.

Keeping all this mind, I decided to engage the children in preparing for
and participating in an artists' exhibition.

I began by introducing the concept of an artist exhibition.
I then asked them the following questions:

What should we include in our exhibition?

What do you think is important for everyone to see?

I wanted them to reflect on what they had done in their art class so far,
and identify things they considered important and which they would like
to share with visitors, or the general public.

The children felt that it was not enough to just exhibit their puppets by
themselves. They felt that their sketches, drawings, writings and other
process work were of equal importance, and needed to be shared as well.

One child pointed out,
"If we only show [the] puppets people will not know we had many ideas."

For student exhibitions, be sure to include at least one artwork from each child.
In other words, every child in the class should be represented. If a child has not
completed the final artwork, include a process piece instead. It's very important for
each child to feel like his or her efforts are being recognised.

Many of the children also thought it important to share with the
audience the distinctive personalities that they had crafted for their
puppet characters, as well as the stories that they had concocted.
As one child stated:

"My puppet can live in water and in land. It has a fish body.
It is very kind. It helps everybody. So when Sindhu's puppet will fall
into [the] lake, my puppet will save her. I will tell people this."

What did we do in session 1? What did we do in session 2?

What are some of the differences between a sketch and a drawing?

How did we construct our puppets?

The children responded enthusiastically, as they went over
the previous 11 art sessions:

"First class we look at art, pictures of puppet, drawing, painting…"

"We look at animal photos and we draw. We draw line and shape…"

"Sketch lines [are] broken; drawing lines [are] nice…"

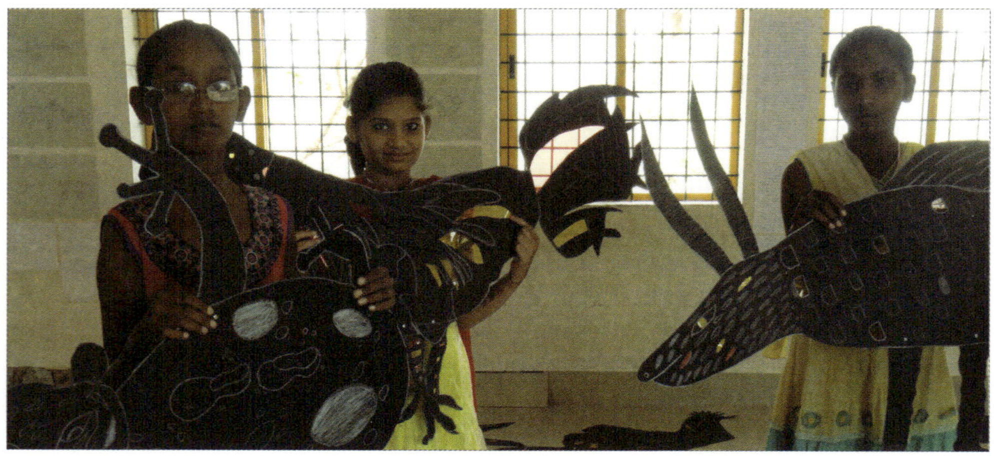

Based on what they remembered, we drew up a list of observations.
We decided that the children could use these as cues, when it came to
sharing their experiences and understanding with visitors to the exhibition.

In addition, the children wanted to practice and perform their stories
for the audience. We discussed the different ways of telling a story.
For example, we discussed how one student in a group could narrate
the story, while the remaining group members could move their puppets
using vigorous gestures to act out the scenes. Alternatively, we talked

about how students within a group could create dialogues for each of their characters, and each student would take their turn in delivering their dialogues.

Through this process of thinking together, the children were able to collaborate, offer support and feedback to one another, and make key decisions.

As a next step, I decided to allocate roles for each of them. I told them that they could rotate these roles amongst themselves during the course of the exhibition. I then went on to outline the roles of an usher, guide and artist. I explained what each of these involved:

An usher keeps an eye out for guests. He or she welcomes them to the exhibition and introduces them to the guide.

A guide is one who takes visitors through the exhibition, and gives them an overall view of all that was done, from one art class to the next.

An artist stands in front of his or her artwork and explains the ideas behind the artwork. An artist also speaks about his or her artistic process.

As the children stepped into these roles, they learned the value of working together. And more important, they realised that they could not think or talk only of what they had done, but they had to connect with what others had done as well.

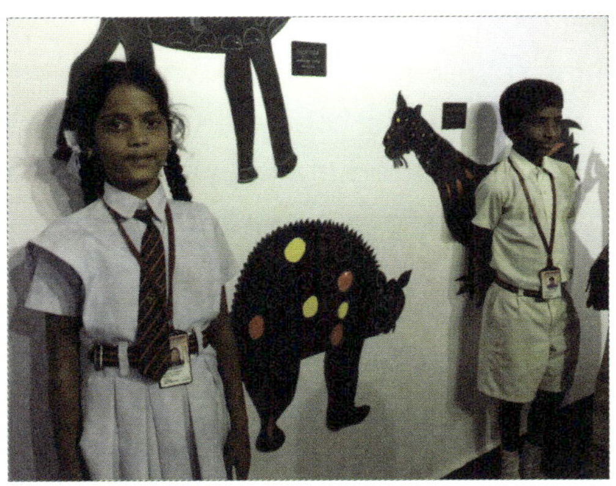
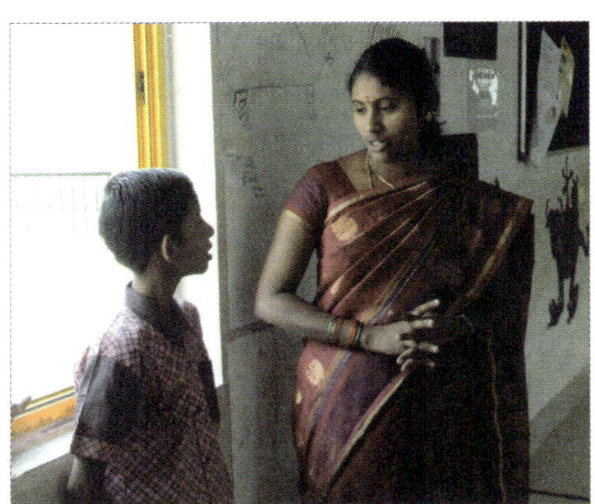

When you plan for the exhibition, make sure that the children take ownership of their ideas. It is important to nurture their confidence—when it comes to responding to what visitors have to say, or to answer questions that are asked of them. This is best done through extensive discussions with the children.

About Art

Artists exhibit in galleries and other public spaces because they want their work to be seen by others. Often their work is presented in such a way that the visitor both views as well as engages with the art. For example, the caption accompanying an artwork could be in the form of a question, to which there is no definite answer. And this means the visitor is expected to formulate his or her own interpretation. The point is to exhibit art in a way that its meanings are accessible to the viewer. Often exhibitions also showcase the artists process and shed light on the complexities and evolution of an artwork, from concept to completion. Children's art could also be displayed in this manner—so that visitors get a clearer picture of the art-making process, the children's experiences of learning, and the decisions they made in order to arrive at their final solutions.

About the Learning Process

There are certain beliefs that people hold when it comes to responding to children's art. A popular belief is that children need positive reinforcement and validation for their work. For example, we often hear a child asking, "Do you like my drawing?" to which the adult responds, "Yes, I love it!" Validating a child's efforts with appreciation, after all, seems like an appropriate thing to do. Some believe that children need guidance, and that responses should focus on helping children understand what needs to be added or adjusted. In other words, offering concrete suggestions that children can apply. Others strongly believe that commenting on a child's artwork can interfere with his or her capacity to be spontaneously expressive. And still others feel that they're not artists, and as such, are not qualified to talk to children about their art.

Children are often habituated to seeking teacher (or parent) approval, relying on the adult's opinion. It is therefore important to help build their capacity to be self-reliant: make their own decisions, reflect on choices made, revisit ideas, and more. Engaging children in a dialogue about their art is a great way of helping build these capacities. However, there are a few important things to keep in mind.

When responding to children's artworks, for example, qualifying remarks such as "That's a beautiful picture" or "I love it" are problematic as they do not help advance children's growth and development in art.

Other points to consider include:

- It is important to give children an opportunity to talk about their own work. Simply asking, "Can you tell me about your artwork," and listening to their responses helps children use language to communicate their intentions. It also allows what is implicit in their work to become explicit.

- When children seek approval for their artwork, it is helpful to point to aspects of their work while talking about what, in your opinion, works well. For example, this is what I said to a child: "I like the way you have made careful selections on which animals to combine, and how. The zebra head, tortoise shell body, rooster legs, and cheetah tail seem to fit well together. The patterns you have added to the various parts of your imaginary animal really helps your puppet stand out."

- One does not have to be an artist to comment on children's art. Instead, one needs to be able to observe the artwork, and describe exactly what is seen, whether commenting on different types of lines used, shapes, colours, or anything else present in the work. Acknowledging, in concrete terms, what children have accomplished can help build within them a recognition of their own ability to make thoughtful choices and combine their choices in interesting ways.

ELEMENTS OF A STRONG ART PROGRAMME

In order to support meaningful, impactful learning in the art classroom - the kind that generates positive outcomes such as those explored in the previous chapters - it is necessary to create the right circumstances under which this learning can emerge and thrive. To this end, a strong art programme should consist of certain essential components, all of which can play an invaluable role in nurturing this type of learning. The following are important to consider when structuring quality art experiences for children:

Focus on Process & Exploration

While there are many kinds of art programmes, there are two distinct types that we encounter most often. In the first, children are provided with a teacher-directed model to follow. The intent here is for all children to be able to successfully complete the task at hand, and create a finished product. For example: a step-by-step mask-making exercise, following a teacher sample, using a paper plate for the face of a cat, pipe cleaners for the whiskers, cut paper for the ears, and black paint to create the eyes, nose, and mouth. This approach is usually driven by a need to control the end result. The end result here: cat masks that look identical. In the second approach, children are free to do whatever they want. This is driven by a desire to give children the freedom to express themselves, and is backed by a strong belief that any interventions can limit expression.

An alternative approach is one based on the belief that the process of learning is as important as the content to be learned. Distinctly different from a product-based approach, with a sole focus on the pre-determined end result, a process-based approach is rooted in the idea that exploration, experimentation, and inquiry are necessary for children to understand the mechanics of things, and for deep and meaningful learning to emerge. It is, however, important to recognise that a process-based approach is not synonymous with an approach that lacks structure—a do-whatever-you-want type of approach.

Some defining characteristics of a process-based approach include:

- Provision of ample opportunities for children to test and manipulate materials to develop a familiarity with the materials, and help them discover what the materials can and cannot do for them. For example, providing opportunities to explore the quality of an artist pencil, explore lines and shapes in sketching and drawing, explore textures and patterns that can be represented with the pencil. Ideas often do not emerge in vacuum, but instead, develop over time, with a deeper understanding of the materials and their capacity to make ideas come to life.

- An emphasis on the individual steps versus a sole focus on the end result. This is driven by a belief that a focus on steps that involve and nurture ideation, investigation, planning, reflection, problem solving, and more, is far more powerful than a narrow focus on creating a finished artwork. This also helps ensures that the finished work distinctly reflects each child's experiences with the process, the choices they've made as a result, and their own unique points of view.

- Provision of multifarious opportunities for continuous growth and development, meeting the children where they're at. In other words, in the case of children who may have more sustained prior experiences with art-making, this approach enables them to revisit familiar art materials, and make new and more nuanced discoveries. For example, children who may have worked with collage before, exploring cut and torn shapes and how they can be combined in different yet interesting ways, may find themselves revisiting collage, this time, however, focusing on exploring the representation of texture, both physical and visual. This is not too dissimilar from how a professional artist might engage with art-making. For children who are new to art-making and have limited prior experiences, this approach enables them to test out the materials without being bogged down by the need to create something that looks "perfect."

- An emphasis on enabling children, over time, to independently arrive at their own unique solutions through a process of experimentation and discovery.

Sequence Learning Experiences

Very often we encounter educational programming that's intent on delivering a lot of information. Children are introduced to new information during every session. And they often have little opportunity to apply what they have learned, reflect on the outcomes, revisit concepts, and build upon them over time, in an effort to develop deep understanding. This is justified by a range of claims: there is too much content to cover; there's not enough time to dwell on specific aspects of the curriculum; a lot can be covered in one class session; children should be exposed to a range of information. Some of these assumptions are held in art as well. Art programmes, in the name of offering a range of experiences, often jump from painting a landscape in one session, to creating a mask in the next, to creating a collage in the third. In the context of the Indian education system, it is important to recognise that in many instances this rapid transfer of knowledge has compromised meaningful student engagement and development of rich insights.

Sequential learning can help remedy this situation. All new learning emerges from prior learning and understanding, and the interactions between the two. This is applicable to all content areas, including the arts. Keeping this in mind, in the art classroom this means that lessons should be thoughtfully sequenced, building from one lesson to the next with a clear end goal in mind. And, children should be given, first and foremost, ample and structured opportunities to explore and experiment with the art materials and techniques introduced. Through their manipulations of a given material (e.g. clay) children gain new insights and understanding about an artistic medium (i.e. sculpture) that they can then apply towards the creation of their artwork. Implementing thoughtfully sequenced lessons, that employ a multi-step process that extends over a period of time, enables children to revisit their artworks and apply their growing understanding of materials in increasingly complex ways. It also offers children continuity in their learning as they move towards the end goal.

Build Visual Literacy

The richness of India's artistic traditions is indisputable. Art is a way of knowing and being in many communities across India. It is an integral part of the day-to-day life of many. We also find that in this present era, visuals are everywhere. Information is transmitted not just with the help of the written word, but through visuals as well. The capacity to read visuals can help transcend, for many, the limitations of traditional language literacy.

Yet, our views about engaging with, and looking at visuals are often limited. While some believe that viewing artworks can inhibit children, as they may feel inadequate in comparison to the artist they're looking at, others see it as an opportunity to offer children a concrete model to follow. In both instances, viewing artworks is seen merely as a way of imparting skill in art.

Given the multiplicity of visual information that surrounds us, the ability for children to make meaning of what they see is an important skill to nurture. Visual literacy involves building in children the capacity to observe carefully, identify details, and use the observed visual information to read an image. Close observation and identification of details are important skills in a wide variety of disciplines. The capacity to read an image and make meaning out of the complex interrelationships between the various component parts requires higher order skills such as critical thinking. Critical thinking also has implications for student success and learning.

Other skills enhanced through the development of visual literacy that have an impact on children's learning, include, the ability to analyse, interpret, offer evidence in support of one's claims, and more. If we acknowledge that speaking and listening should precede reading and writing when acquiring a new language - versus the popular order of writing, reading, listening, and speaking adopted in many schools across India - visual literacy can serve as a stepping stone to acquiring traditional language literacy.

Possible Challenges to Implementing a Quality Art Programme

There are several potential challenges that one may encounter when trying to implement a robust art programme for children—one that is impactful to their learning. But these challenges are far from insurmountable. Recognising these challenges and coming up with concrete strategies is fundamental to overcoming these very challenges.

Art as Secondary

A limited understanding of the value of art, as it relates to children's learning, can get in the way of implementing an enriching art programme. It often results in art being positioned as secondary to other subjects within the school curriculum, if not entirely excluded. And, classifications such as co-scholastic and co-curricular often continue to justify this secondary position accorded to art. It is important to note that advocacy efforts for the inclusion of art in education are more prevalent now in India than they have ever been before. And these efforts are generating awareness regarding the impact of art on children's learning. Art education advocates must, however, become more skillful in making a sound case for the inclusion of art as an integral part of children's learning. While discussions that revolve around the inherent value of art are important and must continue, by themselves, they're not enough. Shedding light on the cognitive benefits associated with art-making, its impact on developing creative thinking abilities, as well as other essential thinking skills and attitudes that enhance children's capacities, are essential in ensuring the inclusion of art, and its elevation within schools.

Art as a Perk

Art programmes that are only about teaching technique, those that believe in non-intervention, and still others that categorise art as fun, expressive, emotional, not work that involves complex thinking processes, are problematic. Such programmes can often diminish the perceived value of art. Art in these instances is often viewed as a perk, not a necessity within schools. And, these limiting perceptions get in the way of broad implementation of art programming for all children across all schools. In order to ensure the inclusion of art within schools, and elevate the position of art education, it is critical to implement quality art programmes that reveal the richness of learning embedded in the art experiences. To start with, it may be helpful for art educators to define clearly what quality in art education looks like (both in terms of programme delivery and outcomes), versus what it isn't. Research on diverse and effective art education practices can provide valuable insights which, when considered in relation to the context for implementation, can yield more intentional and meaningful outcomes.

Limited Time

Limited allocations of time within the school curriculum also pose a challenge to implementing quality art programming. For example, a school may just have one day a week, and one class period, allotted for students to engage with art. In order for meaningful learning to emerge in the art classroom it is beneficial for sufficient time to be allotted towards art-making. Deep and meaningful learning of any kind is a process that emerges over a period of time. One way for art educators to cope with the issue of time is to take on a less-is-more approach when structuring learning experiences in art. In other words, rather than packing in multiple one-off art activities that offer little depth and no real continuity from one session to the next, a more effective strategy is to carefully sequence structured learning experiences that provide opportunities for sustained work with a given art medium over a period of time. Such an approach would enable children to explore and experiment with materials and techniques, and apply their growing understanding to their own work in increasingly complex ways. It would also allow children to reflect on the choices they've made, offer and receive feedback, as well as revisit and modify their work over a period of time.

Lack of Training

A lack of trained art teachers is also a challenge to implementing meaningful art programming. In order to be able to tap into the rich learning embedded in art experiences, an understanding of what this learning looks like coupled

with the knowledge of how to structure meaningful experiences in art
and how to effectively guide children through the process of learning,
is important. An understanding of art materials and artistic practice is
also important. Professional development opportunities can go a long
way in preparing teachers for teaching art, offering them several strategies
to facilitate deep and meaningful engagement. Hands-on professional
development in particular, especially those that offer teachers an
opportunity to explore and experiment with materials and techniques,
as well as experience art-making as their students would, are valuable in
offering teachers a nuanced understanding of the learning embedded in
art experiences, and their impact on students.

Bringing in artists and art educators to schools, pairing them up with
existing teachers is another strategy that can help boost the quality of the
art experiences offered. While artists and art educators bring to the table
a deep understanding of artistic practice and knowledge of materials,
teachers bring an understanding of their students as well as their teaching
practice. Volunteers who have received hands-on training in working
with various artist materials and techniques, structuring art experiences,
implementing carefully developed art curricula, and engaging children
to facilitate their learning, can serve as viable alternatives.

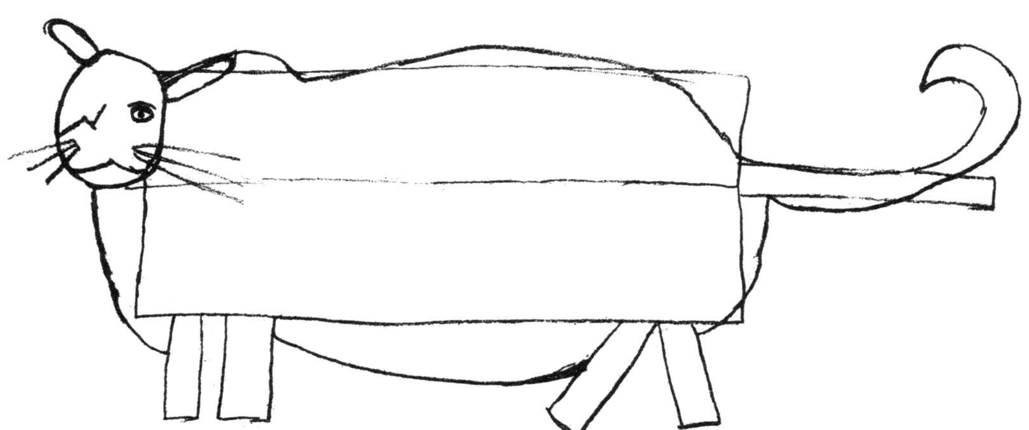

GOING FORWARD

When we talk about educating our children it is essential for us to consider their all-round development, and recognise the role that art plays in nurturing this development. The value quality art programmes offer to children's learning is undeniable. A careful analysis of such programmes and the outcomes they generate over time reveals this. While the range of art experiences available, their differing levels of quality, lack of evaluation mechanisms, and more, can often obscure the rich and meaningful contributions art makes towards children's learning, there are efforts that can be taken to move forward in establishing art as a valuable and necessary part of all children's education. They include:

- Documenting, evaluating, and disseminating best practices that serve as examples of quality teaching and learning in art—examples that can widely influence and inspire more robust art education practice. However, there is first a need to clearly define what quality art education involves, and distinguish it from what it doesn't.

- Encouraging research based on documented best practices set within the Indian education context.

- Developing and sharing teaching and learning resources based on existing research as well as documented best practices.

- Highlighting specific school-based efforts - both independent efforts as well as those in collaboration with external art education organisations - and promoting best practices emerging from within school settings, including the outcomes resulting from those practices. This can go a long way in making an effective case for the inclusion of art within schools.

- Seeking out or creating opportunities to promote awareness regarding the value and impact of art on children's learning. In doing so, it is important to draw attention to not just the intrinsic value of art (i.e. the development of aesthetic awareness, expression, etc.) but also the instrumental or external value, in particular, the impact of art on the cognitive development of children—the development of valuable thinking skills and attitudes. Conferences, exhibitions and workshops are great ways to engage the various stakeholders (parents, educators, the art community, general public, policy makers, and more), and get the word out.

- Supporting teacher training efforts as well as the professional development of artists, volunteers, and community activists, with a commitment to improving the quality of teaching and learning in and through art.

APPENDIX

	UNIT BREAKDOWN (LESSON OBJECTIVE)	MATERIALS LIST
LESSON 1	Students will broaden their views about art. Students will also be able to recognise line and shape as the basis of all form, and create sketches of observed lines and shapes that make up the animal forms in the reference images provided.	• Images of a variety of artworks (sketch, drawing, painting, sculpture, mixed media art, puppets, kolam, etc.) • White printer paper • 3B drawing pencils • Reference images of animals
LESSON 2	Students will be able to create detailed observational drawings of a variety of animals by mapping out simple lines and shapes identified in the reference images first, and adding defining details on top.	• Images of a sketch and a drawing • White printer paper • 3B drawing pencils • Reference images of animals
LESSON 3	Students will be able to selectively combine animal forms, using the reference images provided, to create at least two or more different sketches of imaginary hybrid animals.	• Images of hybrid animals • Newsprint paper • 3B drawing pencils • Reference images of animals
LESSON 4	Students will be able to select one of their hybrid animal sketches, consider any modifications, and create an enlarged, detailed drawing of the same.	• Newsprint paper • 3B drawing pencils • Reference images of animals
LESSON 5	Students will be able to start their hybrid animal puppets by first drawing the body (torso only) of their hybrid animals, while considering and adding select surface patterns, onto thick black construction paper.	• Detail/close-up images of animal hides • Black construction paper • White drawing pencils • Reference images of animals
LESSON 6	Students will be able to draw the head of their hybrid animals, while considering and adding select surface patterns, onto thick black construction paper, keeping in mind proportional relationships between the head and torso.	• Detail/close-up images of animal hides • Black construction paper • White drawing pencils • Reference images of animals

	UNIT BREAKDOWN (LESSON OBJECTIVE)	MATERIALS LIST
LESSON 7	Students will be able to draw the various appendages (legs, tails, wings, fins, etc.) of their hybrid animals, while considering and adding select surface patterns, onto the thick black construction paper, keeping in mind proportional relationships between the appendages, torso, and head.	• Black construction paper • White drawing pencils • Reference images of animals
LESSON 8	Students will be able to cut out the larger forms (head, torso, and appendages) of their hybrid animal puppets.	• Scissors
LESSON 9	Students will be able to selectively cut out patterned details from the surface of their puppet parts.	• Scissors • Hole punchers • Paper cutters
LESSON 10	Students will be able to attach the various parts of their hybrid animal puppets, using brads for at least two moveable parts, and glue for the remaining immoveable parts. Students will also be able to affix supports (popsicle sticks) to the backs of their puppets, to help keep their puppets upright.	• Brads • Glue (Fevicol) • Popsicle sticks
LESSON 11	Students will be able to develop, in small collaborative group settings, a simple story involving their imaginary hybrid animal puppet characters. Students will also be able to practice narrating their stories.	• Sample story and animation stills • White printer paper • Pencils
LESSON 12	Students will be able to plan, execute, and actively participate in an artist exhibition featuring their work.	• Tape • Signage • Final puppets and process artworks (i.e. sketches & drawings) • Written stories

GLOSSARY

- **Art**: Visual art and design that includes drawing, painting, collage, sculpture, printmaking, puppet-making, graphic design, product design, stop-motion animation, photography, and more

- **Sculpture**: Three dimensional artworks made of paper, clay, wire, recyclables, papier-mache, naturally occurring objects, cloth, foam, mixed media, and more

- **Puppet-making:** Creating puppets using a variety of media such as cloth, clay, papier mache, etc. For the purpose of this book, creating shadow puppets using black construction paper, white pencils, brads, glue, ice-cream sticks, and cellophane for details

- **Materials**: Art materials used to create artworks, ranging from traditional art materials such as paint, pencils, clay, collage, etc. to found materials such plastics, cardboard, etc., to natural materials such as twigs, acorns, pebbles, etc., and more

- **Line**: A long and thin stroke or mark made with a pencil on the surface of paper

- **Shape**: The arrangement of lines in a particular way coming together to create an enclosed form. Shapes can refer to geometric shapes (circle, oval, square, rectangle, trapezoid, triangle, etc.); organic shapes (free form or irregular shapes); 2D shapes or 3D shapes

- **Form:** The external appearance of something (e.g. form of the human body, a chair, a tree, etc.)

- **Sketch**: A simple, quickly-rendered, and rough plan for a drawing, often made lightly as a preliminary study

- **Mapping**: Laying down on paper a rough structural foundation for a more detailed drawing to go on top

- **Drawing**: A detailed image that represents something, created using a pencil, combining a series of lines and shapes

- **Observation:** Looking closely and paying attention to details, noticing and perceiving things deeply

- **Imagination:** The capacity to formulate inventive and original ideas in the mind before they take a specific form

- **Hybrid animal**: A unique and imaginative combination of two or more animals

- **Shadow puppet:** A flat puppet (usually figurative), made traditionally out of animal hide, with detailed cutouts on the surface of the puppet. When held between a source of light and a screen, shadow puppets cast an intricate shadow.

- **Detail:** The small features of something that helps give it more information

- **Texture**: The surface quality of something, and how it feels to touch (e.g. rough, smooth, soft, etc.)

- **Pattern**: A decorative surface design made up of repeating lines, shapes, and/or marks

- **Scale**: Increasing or decreasing the size of something (e.g. scaling up or down a drawing)

- **Measurement**: Finding out the dimensions of something (how big or small it is)

- **Proportion**: The comparative size of something in relation to something else

- **Brad**: A metal fastener to hold moving elements of a puppet together

- **Attachment**: Bringing two pieces together securely

- **Moveable**: Something that is capable of being moved

- **Immoveable**: Something that is stationary and incapable of being moved

- **Storytelling**: The act of telling a story, keeping in mind the elements of a story such as plot, sequence, characters, and setting

- **Character:** People, animals, real, imaginary, playing various roles within a story

- **Plot:** The overall plan or storyline of a story that unfolds as a sequence of events

- **Setting:** The place or environment (real or imaginary) where a story occurs

PHOTO CREDITS

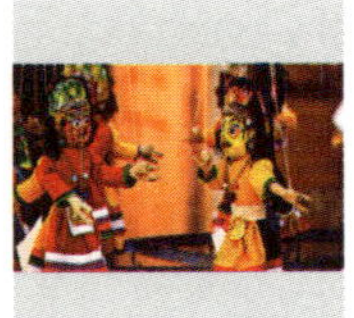

Image 1, page 12

By Sagar Dani

From Unsplash

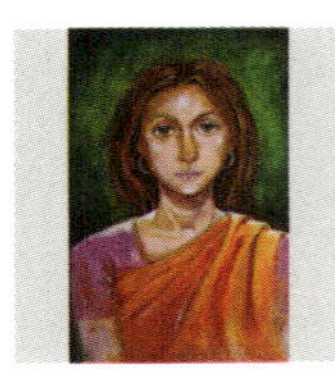

Image 7, page 15

By Aartay Mehta

From Resilience

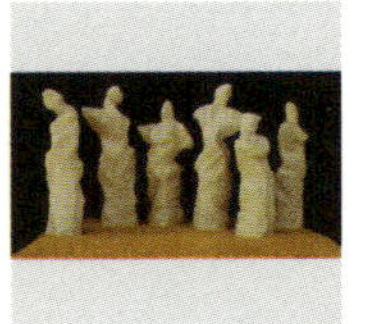

Image 2, page 13

By Eric Gordon Gill

Plaster of Paris
Height variable:
16 in to 22 in

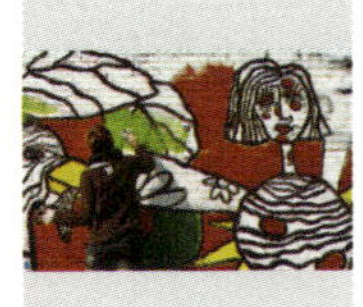

Image 8, page 15

By Amandine Cornillon

From Unsplash

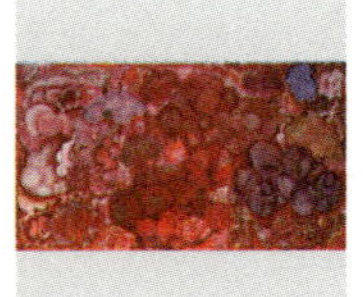

Image 3, page 13

By Nirali Lal

A Pink Cloud Fantasy
48 x 84 inches
Oil on Canvas

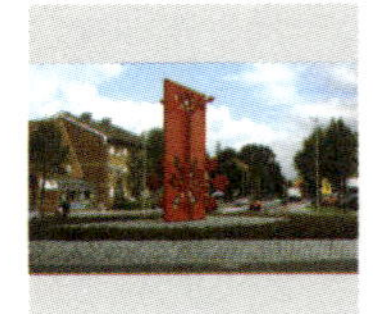

Image 9, page 17

By Josef Zutelgte

Rote Telge, 2006, Steel
8 m x 6 m x 5.5 m

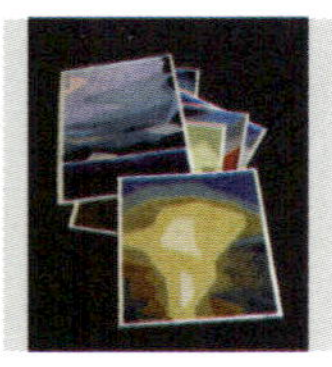

Image 4, page 13

By Ardis Strong

Sunset Sketches

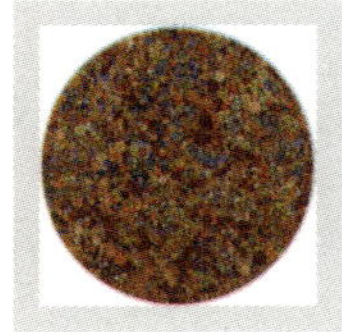

Image 10, page 18

By Hadieh M. Shafie

20900 Pages; Ink &
Acrylic on Paper, 48 in
diameter x 3.5 in deep

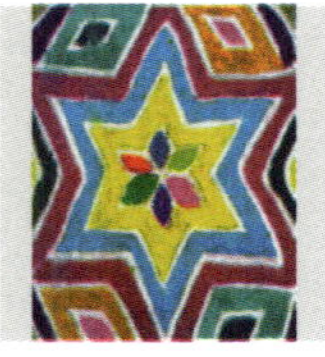

Image 5, page 14

From Tara Books'
Archive

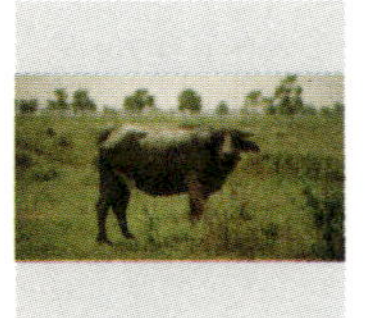

Image 11, page 27

By Min An

From Pexels

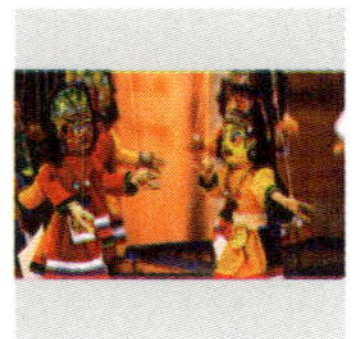

Image 6, page 14

By Sagar Dani

From Unsplash

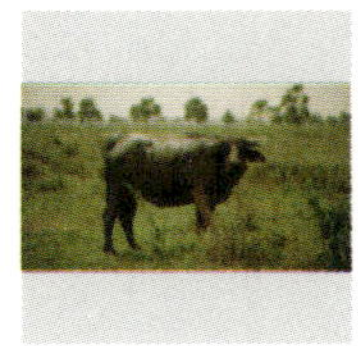

Image 12, page 28

By Min An

From Pexels

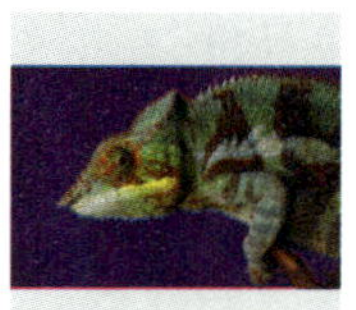

Image 13, page 33

By Pierre Bamin

From Unsplash

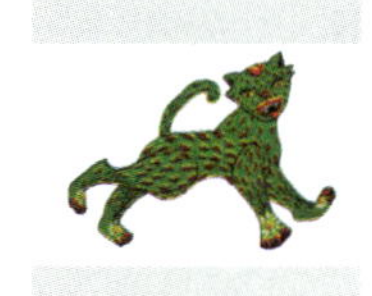

Image 19, page 53

By Polina

Polina the Jaguar

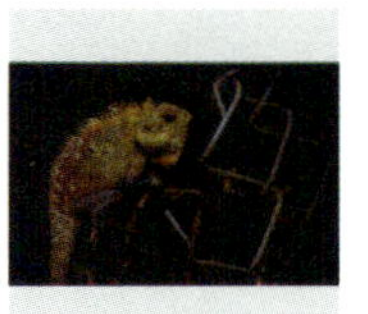

Image 14, page 35

By Himesh Kumar Behera

From Unsplash

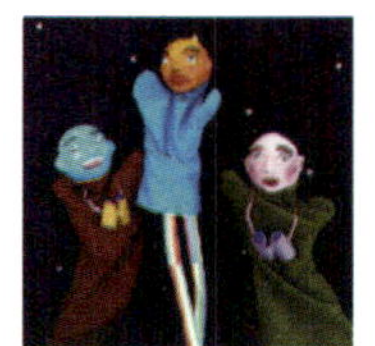

Image 20, page 53

By Polina

Bunka and Pancha

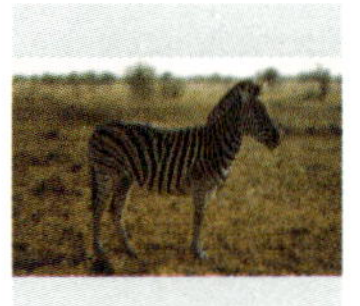

Image 15, page 37

By Adriaan Greyling

From Pexels

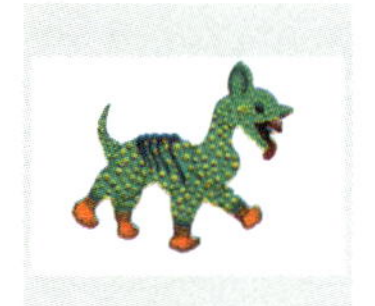

Image 21, page 54

By Polina

Polina the Dog

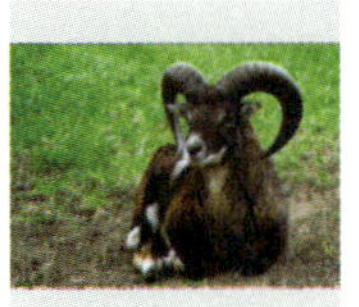

Image 16, page 38

By Dusan Smetana

From Unsplash

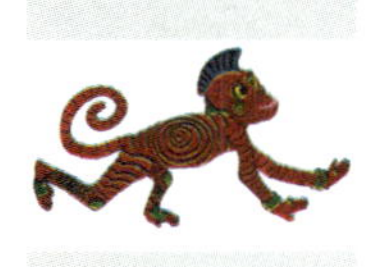

Image 22, page 55

By Polina

Polina the Monkey

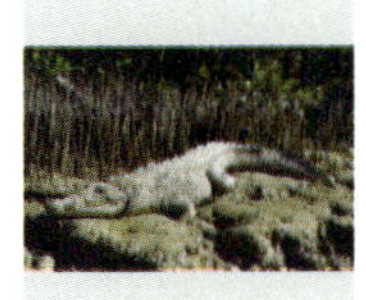

Image 17, page 39

By Bradley Feller

From Unsplash

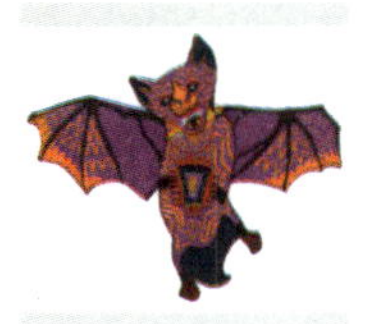

Image 22, page 55

By Polina

Polina the Bat

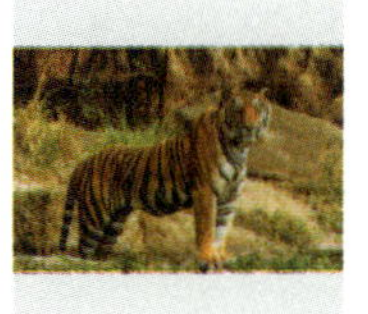

Image 18, page 40

By A G

From Unsplash

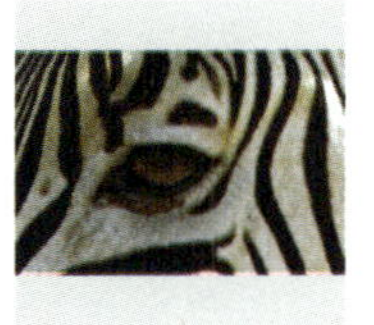

Image 23, page 64

By Magda Ehlers

From Pexels

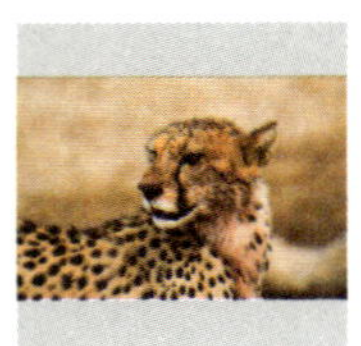

Image 24, page 65

By Rodrigo Ardilha

From Unsplash

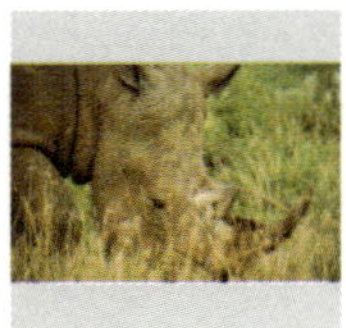

Image 25, page 65

By Frans Van Heerden

From Unsplash

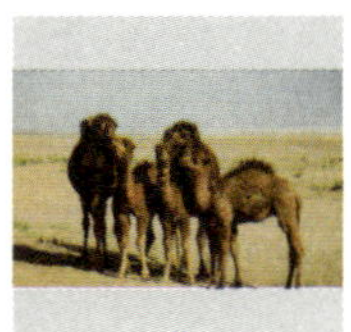

Image 26, page 66

By Steven Su

From Unsplash

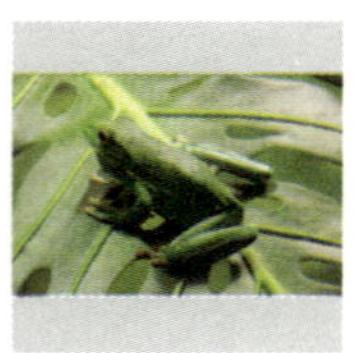

Image 27, page 66

By Joel Henry

From Unsplash

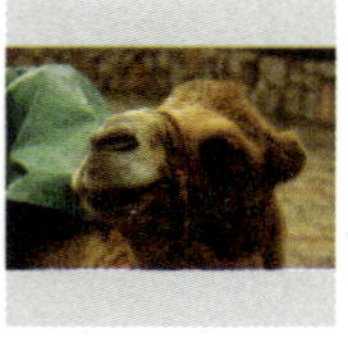

Image 28, page 68

By Steven Su

From Unsplash

Photographs by Nisha Nair

Pages 49, 50, 56, 57, 61, 62, 92, 93

Artwork by Nisha Nair

Pages 22, 23, 29, 35, 44, 46, 47, 67, 69, 81

Artwork by children

Cover, back cover, endsheets, copyright page, title page, acknowledgements

Pages 9, 30, 31, 36, 37, 38, 39, 40, 48, 49, 50, 58, 59, 60, 70, 71, 77, 78, 79, 82, 83, 84, 85, 86, 87, 88, 89, 103